moda All-Stars

Top the Table

17 QUILT PATTERNS FOR RUNNERS, TOPPERS, AND MORE!

COMPILED BY **Lissa Alexander**

Martingale®
Create with Confidence

Moda All-Stars
Top the Table: 17 Quilt Patterns for Runners, Toppers, and More!
© 2021 by Martingale & Company®

Martingale®
18939 120th Ave NE, Suite 101
Bothell, WA 98011-9511 USA
ShopMartingale.com

Printed in Hong Kong
26 25 24 23 22 21   8 7 6 5 4 3 2 1

Library of Congress Cataloging-in-Publication Data is available upon request.

ISBN: 978-1-68356-114-9

MISSION STATEMENT

We empower makers who use fabric and yarn to make life more enjoyable.

CREDITS

PUBLISHER AND
CHIEF VISIONARY OFFICER
Jennifer Erbe Keltner

CONTENT DIRECTOR
Karen Costello Soltys

DESIGN MANAGER
Adrienne Smitke

MANAGING EDITOR
Tina Cook

PRODUCTION MANAGER
Regina Girard

ACQUISITIONS AND
DEVELOPMENT EDITOR
Laurie Baker

COVER AND
BOOK DESIGNER
Kathy Kotomaimoce

TECHNICAL WRITER
Nancy Mahoney

PHOTOGRAPHERS
Adam Albright
Brent Kane

COPY EDITOR
Sheila Chapman Ryan

ILLUSTRATOR
Sandy Loi

SPECIAL THANKS
*Photography for this book was taken at the homes of:
Tracie Fish in Bothell, Washington, and
Libby Warnken in Ankeny, Iowa.*

What's your creative passion?

Find it at **ShopMartingale.com**

books • eBooks • ePatterns • blog • free projects
videos • tutorials • inspiration • giveaways

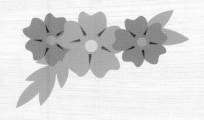

Contents

Introduction

Gather 'round the table! It's a bidding many of us call out to family and friends as they get together in our homes. And often it's those same folks seated around our tables who fill our lives with great shared memories of time spent with one another. For quilters, a table topper or runner is the perfect finishing touch to a well-dressed table. Whether casual or formal, it's a nod to the hobby we love as well as a warm inviting touch.

By now, many of the Moda All-Stars may seem like friends. In various combinations, they've joined forces to do good, donating royalties from 10 previous Moda All-Stars series titles to a variety of charitable causes. The book you're reading is no exception. Royalties from this book are going to Action Against Hunger, the leader in a global movement that aims to end life-threatening hunger for good within our lifetimes (ActionAgainstHunger.org).

And since quilters can become fast friends (even when meeting for the first time), we know you'll enjoy learning more about each of these fabulous designers in the Table Talk section alongside each project.

So, gather your favorite fabrics and maybe a cup of coffee or tea, and linger over the following pages to choose which runner or topper you'll make first. We know the next time family and friends gather 'round your table, they'll be dazzled by your latest creation!

~Lissa Alexander

Happy Days

You scream, I scream, we all scream for table toppers! An easy table runner starts with 5" squares and ends with a beautifully adorned table and a smile on your face.

SHERRI L. McCONNELL

FINISHED TABLE RUNNER
21½" × 42¾"

Materials

Yardage is based on 42"-wide fabric.

60 squares, 5" × 5", of assorted prints for blocks
¼ yard of white solid for setting triangles
⅜ yard of mint print for border
⅓ yard of red print for binding
1⅜ yards of fabric for backing
28" × 49" piece of batting

Cutting

All measurements include ¼"-wide seam allowances.

From *each* 5" square, cut:
3 rectangles, 1½" × 5" (180 total)

From the white solid, cut:
6 squares, 5½" × 5½"; cut each square into quarters
   diagonally to make 24 side setting triangles
   (2 are extra)
2 squares, 3" × 3"; cut each square in half diagonally
   to make 4 corner setting triangles

From the mint print, cut:
4 strips, 2½" × 42"; crosscut into:
   2 strips, 2½" × 38¾"
   2 strips, 2½" × 21½"

From the red print, cut:
4 strips, 2¼" × 42"

Making the Blocks

Press all seam allowances in the direction indicated by the arrows.

Randomly sew three 1½" × 5" rectangles together along the long edges. Trim the block to 3½" square, including seam allowances. Repeat to make a total of 60 blocks.

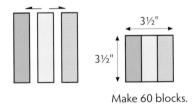

Make 60 blocks.

Assembling the Table Runner

1 Refer to the table-runner assembly diagram on page 9 to lay out the blocks and white setting triangles in diagonal rows. Sew the pieces in each row together. Join the rows. Add the corner setting triangles last. The table-runner center should measure 17½" × 38¾", including seam allowances.

Table Talk
SHERRI L. McCONNELL

How many chairs are around your most-often-used table? Four.

If you could sit around the table with two or three other quilters, who would they be and why?
Lissa Alexander (she's so knowledgeable about mixing prints, patterns, and colors in her scrap quilt designs); Barbara Brackman (she's an encyclopedia of quilting. I'd love to meet her in person); and Susan Ache (she's so prolific, I'd enjoy visiting with her).

What's something you know you do differently from most people? I cut up scraps to use later while cutting out a project. I think this comes from my years of sewing for other people!

Describe your favorite way to set your table.
My grandmother loved beautiful dishes, as did my husband's grandmother, so we have many beautiful dishes. I use them all the time.

What grabs your attention most when you're looking at quilts? The design and block settings. I love when I have to think a bit to figure it all out!

What's your favorite occasion that causes people to gather around your table? Christmas first, but Thanksgiving is a close second. William Bradford, a governor of Plymouth Colony, was my direct 11th great-grandfather, so I've always loved Thanksgiving.

When was the last time you tried something new and what was it? I tried raw tuna for the first time and actually liked it.

Name one thing you always like to have on your table. Fancy napkins. I think this comes from my grandmother, who also loved beautiful napkins and napkin rings.

When quilting a small project: I try to remind myself that finished is better than perfect. I'm not fabulous at either machine or hand quilting, but I do love trying and practicing both.

AQuiltingLife.com

2 Sew the mint 2½" × 38¾" strips to the long edges of the table-runner center. Sew the mint 2½" × 21½" strips to the short ends of the table runner. The table runner should measure 21½" × 42¾".

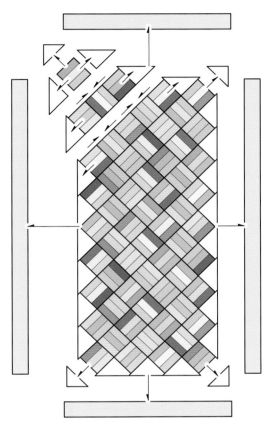

Table-runner assembly

Finishing the Table Runner

For more details on any finishing steps, visit ShopMartingale.com/HowtoQuilt for free downloadable information.

1 Layer the table-runner top with batting and backing; baste the layers together.

2 Quilt by hand or machine. The table runner shown is machine quilted with an allover swirling design.

3 Use the red 2¼"-wide strips to make binding and then attach the binding to the table runner.

Designed and pieced by
SHERRI L. McCONNELL;
quilted by MARION BOTT

Charmingly Recycled

That old pair of jeans you've been waiting to fit back into for years? Ditch the guilt and have fun cutting them up for a charming little table topper that you'll never outgrow!

LISA BONGEAN

FINISHED TABLE TOPPER
12½" × 12½"

Materials

Yardage is based on 42"-wide fabric.

½ yard *total* of old denim jeans or denim fabric for blocks*

25 squares, 2½" × 2½", of assorted gray-and-white prints for blocks

¼ yard of gray-and-white floral for binding

Template plastic

Fine-tip permanent marker

*If using recycled jeans, you'll need 1 to 2 pairs of 100% cotton jeans (depending on the size of the jeans). If you want a variety of blues in your table topper, you'll need several pairs.

Cutting

All measurements include ¼"-wide seam allowances.

From the gray-and-white floral, cut:
2 strips, 2¼" × 42"

Assembling the Table Topper

Press all seam allowances in the direction indicated by the arrows.

1 Trace the circle pattern on page 13 onto template plastic. Cut out the template directly on the drawn line.

2 Use the circle template and permanent marker to trace 25 circles on the wrong side of the denim. Cut out the circles directly on the drawn lines.

3 Center a print square on a denim circle, wrong sides together. Stitch diagonally across the square in both directions to form an X.

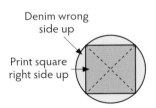

Denim wrong side up

Print square right side up

Make 25 circles.

4 Layer two circles from step 3, denim sides together, and stitch along one edge of the squares. Press the resulting arcs open and stitch ⅛" from the curved raw edges.

Stitch.

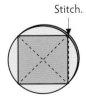
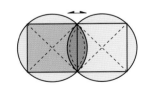

Table Talk
LISA BONGEAN

How many chairs are around your most-often-used table? Eight.

If you could sit around the table with two or three other quilters, who would they be and why?
Any quilter! I find all quilters interesting. I love meeting new quilters, as well as veteran quilters. I learn from them all. But, if you're making me choose one, I guess it would be Bonnie Hunter. I feel like we have somewhat parallel lives, and I would love to see if our personalities are similar as well.

What's something you know you do differently from most people? I can look at one thing and it says something else to me, sparking another idea.

Describe your favorite way to set your table.
We're a buffet family. We make lots of food and set it out for all to choose what they love. We always have way too much food and then argue over who gets to take what home with them. My mom is a great cook and holds us all together with her love of food and family.

What grabs your attention most when you're looking at quilts? I guess it's the pattern. I love quilt patterns. I love dissecting them, like a good mystery. Instead of *who* did it, *how* did they do that? Is there an easier way?

What's your favorite occasion that causes people to gather around your table? I love summer and picnics, so I'll say the Fourth of July celebrations!

When was the last time you tried something new and what was it? English paper piecing without using any glue to turn the edges.

Name one thing you always like to have on your table. Now, this is a silly question. A quilt, of course!

When quilting a small project: I keep the scale of the quilting small as well. I love to just stitch ¾" or ½" grids on my pieced table toppers and small quilts.

LisaBongean.com
PrimitiveGatherings.us

5 Repeat step 4 to make five rows of five circles each.

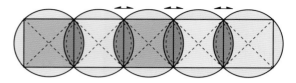

Make 5 rows.

6 Join the rows, stitching along the edges of the print squares. Press the denim arcs open; stitch ⅛" from the curved raw edges. Clip the raw edges of the stitched denim arcs, stopping one or two threads from the stitched line, so they will fray when washed.

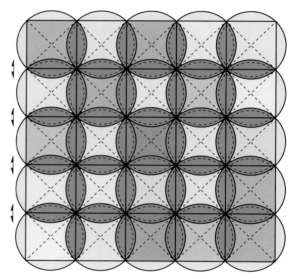

Table-topper assembly

7 Trim the outer denim edges even with the edges of the print squares. The table topper should measure 12½" square.

Trim even with print squares.

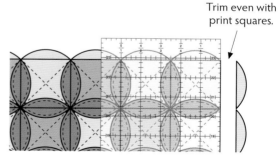

8 Use the gray-and-white floral 2¼"-wide strips to make binding; attach the binding to the topper. Machine wash and dry to fray the denim arc edges.

Designed and made by
LISA BONGEAN

Circle
Cut 25 from
denim.

Farmhouse Geese

Fly through the piecing of a sweet little runner, then find a favorite spot to land while you add the rustic hand-stitched details.

KARLA EISENACH

FINISHED TABLE RUNNER
9" × 33"

Materials

Yardage is based on 42"-wide fabric.

18 rectangles, 2" × 3½" *each*, of assorted black prints for flying-geese units

⅓ yard of cream solid for flying-geese units and inner border

⅜ yard of black print for outer border and binding

⅜ yard of fabric for backing

13" × 37" piece of batting

#10 cream crochet thread

Size 6 embroidery needle

Cutting

All measurements include ¼"-wide seam allowances.

From the cream solid, cut:

2 strips, 2" × 42"; crosscut into 36 squares, 2" × 2"

2 strips, 2½" × 42"; crosscut into:

    2 strips, 2½" × 27½"

    2 strips, 2½" × 7½"

From the black print, cut:

3 strips, 1¼" × 42"; crosscut into:

    2 strips, 1¼" × 31½"

    2 strips, 1¼" × 9"

3 strips, 2¼" × 42"

Assembling the Table Runner

Press all seam allowances in the direction indicated by the arrows.

1 Draw a diagonal line from corner to corner on the wrong side of each cream square. Place a marked square on one end of a black rectangle, right sides together. Sew on the marked line. Trim the excess corner fabric ¼" from the stitched line. Place a marked square on the opposite end of the black rectangle. Sew and trim as before to make a flying-geese unit. Make 18 units measuring 2" × 3½", including seam allowances.

Make 18 units, 2" × 3½".

2 Lay out nine flying-geese units pointing left and nine units pointing right. Join the units to make a row measuring 3½" × 27½", including seam allowances.

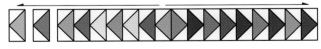

Make 1 row, 3½" × 27½".

3 Refer to the table-runner assembly on page 16 to sew the cream 2½" × 27½" strips to the long

edges of the table runner. Sew the cream 2½" × 7½" strips to the short ends of the table runner. The table runner should measure 7½" × 31½", including seam allowances.

4 Sew the black 1¼" × 31½" strips to the long edges of the table runner. Sew the black 1¼" × 9" strips to the short ends of the table runner. The table runner should measure 9" × 33".

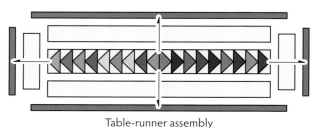

Table-runner assembly

Finishing the Table Runner

For more details on any finishing steps, visit ShopMartingale.com/HowtoQuilt for free downloadable information.

1 Layer the table-runner top with batting and backing; baste the layers together.

2 Use a single strand of crochet thread and the embroidery needle to sew rag stitches (random-length straight stitches) across all the seamlines, stitching through all the layers (top, batting, and backing). Karla's stitches are about ¼" long and spaced about ¼" apart.

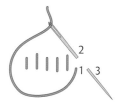

Rag stitch

3 Use the black 2¼"-wide strips to make binding and then attach the binding to the table runner.

Designed and made by
KARLA EISENACH

Table Talk
KARLA EISENACH

How many chairs are around your most-often-used table? Three stools are at the kitchen island.

If you could sit around the table with two or three other quilters, who would they be and why? Anne Sutton, Me and My Sister Designs (two for one, Barb and Mary), and Sandy Klop—they always have great stories to tell.

Describe your favorite way to set your table. I like to set a buffet table when our family is all together.

What grabs your attention most when you're looking at quilts? The first think I notice about quilts is color.

When was the last time you tried something new and what was it? Last year I bought a chop saw. It was a little intimidating, but I made the cutest little wood houses.

Name one thing you always like to have on your table. Plates, silverware, napkins, and water glasses. Not too exciting, I know.

When quilting a small project: I keep in mind the rest of my decor. Even if I'm making something small, I like the pieces throughout my home to coordinate. That means most of what I make is mostly black and white.

TheSweetwaterCo.com

17

Stars at Play

Unlike the stars in the heavens, this trio of twinkling beauties can be enjoyed all day and night. Pick fun fabrics in distinct colors to make your table runner shine bright!

SANDY KLOP

FINISHED TABLE RUNNER
17¾" × 45½"
FINISHED BLOCK
17¼" × 15"

Materials

Yardage is based on 42"-wide fabric. Fat eighths measure 9" × 21".

11 fat eighths of assorted green, gold, red, and navy prints for blocks (referred to collectively as "dark")*
⅜ yard of cream print for setting triangles
3 fat eighths of assorted light prints for blocks
⅓ yard of multicolored stripe for binding
1⅜ yards of fabric for backing
24" × 52" piece of batting
Template plastic
Sandy used 3 green, 3 gold, 3 red, and 2 navy fat eighths.

Cutting

All measurements include ¼"-wide seam allowances.

From the cream print, cut:
2 strips, 5" × 42"

From *each* of the assorted dark prints, cut:
2 strips, 3" × 21"; crosscut into 6 rectangles,
   3" × 5⅜" (66 total)

From *each* of the assorted light prints, cut:
2 strips, 3" × 21"; crosscut into 6 rectangles,
   3" × 5⅜" (18 total)

From the multicolored stripe, cut:
4 strips, 2¼" × 42"

Making the Blocks

Refer to the photo on page 20 for color placement guidance throughout. Press all seam allowances in the direction indicated by the arrows.

1 Place matching dark rectangles right side up on a cutting mat. Cut three dark rectangles in half diagonally from the upper-left corner to the lower-right corner to yield six triangles. Cut the remaining three dark rectangles in half diagonally from the lower-left corner to the upper-right corner to yield six reverse triangles. In the same way, cut the remaining dark and light rectangles in half to make six triangles and six reverse triangles of each print, keeping like triangles together.

Cut 3 each from dark print.

2 To make a block center star, you'll need six triangles and six reversed triangles from one dark print. From two other dark prints, you'll also need three triangles and three reversed triangles. (Notice for the center star, Sandy used six triangles and six reversed triangles from two different dark prints only.) With right sides together, join a triangle and a reversed triangle from two different prints, making sure to orient the triangles as shown. Trace the trimming triangle pattern on page 22 onto template plastic; cut it out. Align the triangle trimming template with the base of

Table Talk
SANDY KLOP

How many chairs are around your most-often-used table? Six chairs, but only three of them are used regularly.

If you could sit around the table with two or three other quilters, who would they be and why? Hands down, my three would be Jennifer Keltner, Elizabeth Beese, and Lissa Alexander.

What's something you know you do differently from most people? My husband says I sew all the time! Is that different from most? I'm not sure?

Describe your favorite way to set your table. I would set the table with a French tablecloth, French dishes, and French glassware.

What grabs your attention most when you're looking at quilts? All I see are the colors. I'm not looking to see if the points are accurate!

What's your favorite occasion that causes people to gather around your table? We don't gather at my table anymore. I passed that baton a long time ago. My dining room table has become the cutting room!

When was the last time you tried something new and what was it? I bought myself an Earthquake rototiller and tore up my front yard!

Name one thing you always like to have on your table. My iPad so I can do a puzzle every day.

AmericanJane.com

Designed and made by
SANDY KLOP

the unit, placing the center line of the template on the seamline. Trim the unit. Make three of each unit.

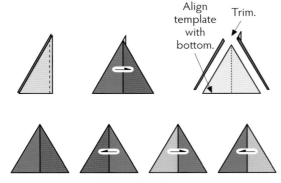

Make 3 of each unit.

3 To complete the hexagon-shaped block, you'll need six triangles and six reversed triangles *each* from one dark print and one light print. Join a dark triangle and a light reversed triangle. Trim the unit as described in step 2. Make six units. Repeat with the dark reversed triangles and light triangles. You'll have 24 dark triangles left over.

Make 6 of each unit.

4 Lay out the units from steps 2 and 3 in four rows, noting the orientation of the units. Sew the units into rows. Join the rows to make a hexagon block. Make three blocks measuring 17¾" × 15½", including seam allowances. Each side of the hexagon should measure 5½", including seam allowances.

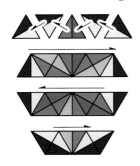

Make 3 blocks, 17¾" × 15½".

Assembling the Table Runner

1 Trace triangle patterns A and B on page 23 onto template plastic. Cut out the triangle templates directly on the traced lines.

2 Using the triangle templates, cut four A triangles and four B triangles from the cream strips.

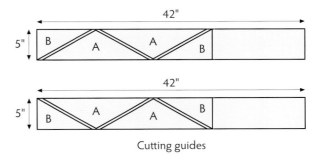

Cutting guides

3 On the wrong side of each cream A triangle, mark the right-angle corner ¼" from the raw edges in preparation for Y-seam construction.

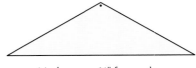

Mark corner ¼" from edge.

4 Join the hexagon blocks as shown in the table-runner assembly diagram on page 22. Sew the cream A triangles to the blocks, starting with a small backstitch at the ¼" mark and sewing to the outside edge. Add cream B triangles to corners last.

5 Trim and square up the table runner, making sure to leave ¼" beyond the points of all blocks for seam allowances. The table runner should measure 17¾" × 45½".

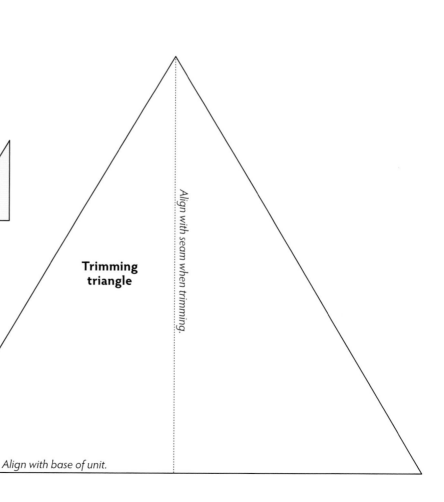

Table-runner assembly

Finishing the Table Runner

For more details on any finishing steps, visit ShopMartingale.com/HowtoQuilt for free downloadable information.

1 Layer the table-runner top with batting and backing; baste the layers together.

2 Quilt by hand or machine. The table runner shown is machine quilted with an allover meandering design.

3 Use the striped 2¼"-wide strips to make binding and then attach the binding to the table runner.

Trimming triangle

Align with seam when trimming.

Align with base of unit.

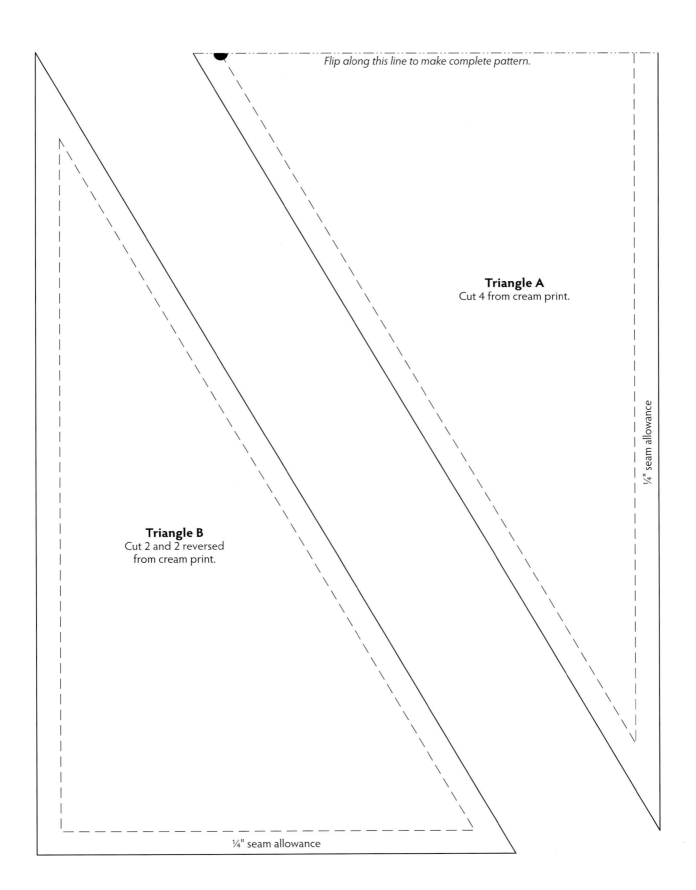

Flip along this line to make complete pattern.

Triangle A
Cut 4 from cream print.

¼" seam allowance

Triangle B
Cut 2 and 2 reversed
from cream print.

¼" seam allowance

Put a Ring on It

It's easy to say "yes" to a bright and cheerful table topper. For a match made in heaven, pair a fun floral with coordinating prints.

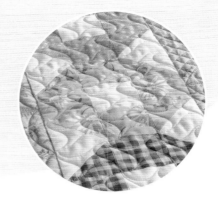

BARBARA GROVES
and MARY JACOBSON

FINISHED TABLE TOPPER
42½" × 42½"
FINISHED BLOCK
6" × 6"

Materials

Yardage is based on 42"-wide fabric.

½ yard of white solid for blocks
16 squares, 10" × 10", of assorted prints for blocks
1⅝ yards of aqua floral for center square and border
½ yard of aqua dot for binding
2¾ yards of fabric for backing
49" × 49" piece of batting

Cutting

All measurements include ¼"-wide seam allowances.

From the white solid, cut:
3 strips, 2⅞" × 42"; crosscut into 32 squares,
    2⅞" × 2⅞"
1 strip, 2½" × 42"; crosscut into 16 squares, 2½" × 2½"

From *each* of the assorted prints, cut:
2 squares, 2⅞" × 2⅞" (32 total)
4 squares, 2½" × 2½" (64 total)

From the aqua floral, cut:
5 strips, 6½" × 42"; cut *2 of the strips*
    to 30½" long
1 square, 18½" × 18½"

From the aqua dot, cut:
5 strips, 2¼" × 42"

Making the Blocks

Press all seam allowances in the direction indicated by the arrows.

1. Draw a diagonal line from corner to corner on the wrong side of each white 2⅞" square. Layer a marked square on a print 2⅞" square, right sides together. Sew ¼" from both sides of the drawn line. Cut the unit apart on the marked line to make two half-square-triangle units. Repeat to make a total of 64 units measuring 2½" square, including seam allowances. Keep like units together.

Make 64 units,
2½" × 2½".

2. Lay out four matching half-square-triangle units, four 2½" squares from the same print as the half-square-triangle units, and one white 2½" square in three horizontal rows. Sew the pieces in each row together. Join the rows to make a block. Repeat to make a total of 16 blocks measuring 6½" square, including seam allowances.

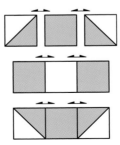 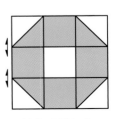

Make 16 blocks,
6½" × 6½".

Assembling the Table Topper

1 Join three blocks to make a side row. Make two rows measuring 6½" × 18½", including seam allowances.

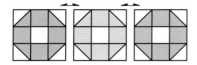

Make 2 side rows,
6½" × 18½".

2 Join five blocks to make the top row. Repeat to make the bottom row. The rows should measure 6½" × 30½", including seam allowances.

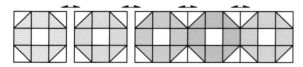

Make 2 top/bottom rows,
6½" × 30½".

3 Refer to the table-topper assembly diagram below to sew the side rows to opposite sides of the aqua floral square. Sew the top and bottom rows to the top and bottom edges. The table-topper center should measure 30½" square, including seam allowances.

4 Sew the aqua floral 6½" × 30½" strips to opposite sides of the table topper.

5 Measure the length of the remaining 6½"-wide aqua strips. If they are at least 42½" long, there is no need to join them. If shorter than 42½", join the remaining aqua floral 6½" × 42" strips end to end. From the pieced strip, cut two 42½"-long strips. Sew these strips to the top and bottom edges of the table topper. The table topper should measure 42½" square.

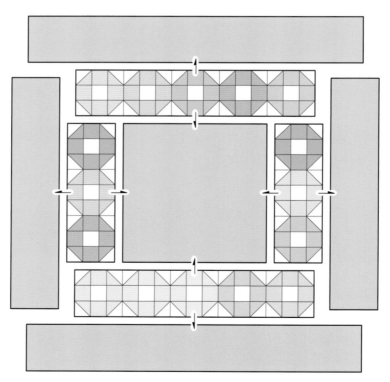

Table-topper assembly

Designed and pieced by
BARBARA GROVES and MARY JACOBSON;
quilted by SHARON ELSBERRY

Finishing the Table Topper

For more details on any finishing steps, visit ShopMartingale.com/HowtoQuilt for free downloadable information.

1 Layer the table-topper top with batting and backing; baste the layers together.

2 Quilt by hand or machine. The table topper shown is machine quilted with curved crosshatching and swirls in the center square and border. A continuous curved-line design is quilted across the blocks.

3 Use the aqua dot 2¼"-wide strips to make binding and then attach the binding to the table topper.

Table Talk
BARBARA GROVES and MARY JACOBSON

The like-minded sisters gave us one set of answers. Guess which answers are from "me" and which are from "my sister."

How many chairs are around your most-often-used table? Three bar stools because we mostly eat at the kitchen island watching TV.

If you could sit around the table with two or three other quilters, who would they be and why? Lissa Alexander—she's my idol! Julie Karasek, shop owner of Patched Works, because she's one of the best businesswomen I know. Jennifer Keltner, because she'd make me laugh until I spit milk out my nose!

Describe your favorite way to set your table. We never use paper plates—I always set the table with plain white ceramic plates and silverware. Foods that were cooked in pans are served in bowls or on platters. I have a great set of buffalo china!

What's something you know you do differently from most people? If we're talking about quilting, I press all my seams open. If we're talking about setting the table, I try not to place bottles on the table. I put condiments in small bowls instead.

What's your favorite occasion that causes people to gather around your table? Thanksgiving and Christmas!

When was the last time you tried something new and what was it you tried? Yesterday I made lasagna roll-ups from a recipe I got on Food Network. I won't be making them again.

Name one thing you always like to have on your table. Fun salt-and-pepper shakers.

When quilting a small project: Keep it simple! If I want something fancier, it goes to my quilter.

MeandMySisterDesigns.com

Summer Nine Patch

The charm of a scrappy table topper is that each patch is different from the next. It's the perfect project to make from your scrap basket or any collection of your favorite fabrics.

JOANNA FIGUEROA

FINISHED TABLE TOPPER
29½" × 29½"
FINISHED BLOCK
3" × 3"

Materials

Yardage is based on 42"-wide fabric.

⅛ yard *total* of assorted scraps from *each* of 8 color families for Nine Patch blocks (referred to collectively as "dark")*

⅓ yard of navy floral for blocks and outer border

¼ yard *each* of 8 assorted cream prints for blocks, setting squares, and outer border

¼ yard of cream dot for inner border

⅓ yard of red gingham for binding

1 yard of fabric for backing

36" × 36" piece of batting

Joanna used blues, reds, yellows, greens, lines, aquas, and oranges.

Cutting

All measurements include ¼"-wide seam allowances.

From *each of 7* of the dark color families, cut:
12 squares, 1½" × 1½" (84 total)

From the remaining color family, cut a *total* of:
16 squares, 1½" × 1½"

From the navy floral, cut:
5 strips, 1½" × 42"; crosscut *1 of the strips* into
    25 squares, 1½" × 1½"

From *each* of the assorted cream prints, cut:
1 strip, 3½" × 42"; crosscut into 3 squares, 3½" × 3½"
    (24 total)
2 strips, 1½" × 42"; *crosscut 1 of the strips* into
    13 squares, 1½" × 1½" (104 total; 4 are extra)

From the cream dot, cut:
4 strips, 1½" × 42"; crosscut into:
    2 strips, 1½" × 23½"
    2 strips, 1½" × 21½"

From the red gingham, cut:
4 strips, 2¼" × 42"

Making the Blocks

Press all seam allowances in the direction indicated by the arrows.

Lay out four assorted dark squares from the same color family, four assorted cream 1½" squares, and one navy square in three horizontal rows of three squares each. Sew the squares in each row together. Join the rows to make a block. Repeat to make a total of 25 blocks measuring 3½" square, including seam allowances.

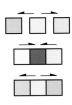

Make 25 blocks,
3½" × 3½".

Making the Border

1 Join one navy and two randomly selected cream 1½"-wide strips as shown to make strip set A. Make two strip sets measuring 3½" × 42", including seam allowances. Crosscut the strip sets into 52 segments, 1½" × 3½".

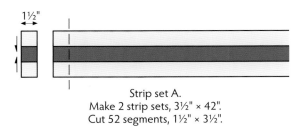

Strip set A.
Make 2 strip sets, 3½" × 42".
Cut 52 segments, 1½" × 3½".

2 Join one navy and two randomly selected cream 1½"-wide strips as shown to make strip set B. Make two strip sets measuring 3½" × 42", including seam allowances. Crosscut the strip sets into 52 segments, 1½" × 3½".

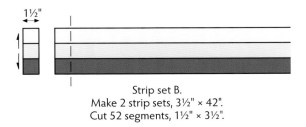

Strip set B.
Make 2 strip sets, 3½" × 42".
Cut 52 segments, 1½" × 3½".

3 Join two B segments and one A segment to make a corner block. Make four blocks measuring 3½" square, including seam allowances.

Make 4 blocks,
3½" × 3½".

Table Talk
JOANNA FIGUEROA

How many chairs are around your most-often-used table? Three kitchen stools at the end of our kitchen counter. Since there are five in our family, someone is always on the floor, on the counter, or pulling up an extra chair!

What's something you know you do differently from most people? Since I taught myself how to quilt on my own and from a book, I learned how to measure and cut fabric using my mat. I know now that I am supposed to be using my ruler, but it's just too late to retrain myself!

Describe your favorite way to set your table. A quilted runner, oversized cream ceramic dishes, various sizes of mason jar glasses, little herb and garden flower bouquets, and vintage silverware that my mom found at a flea market before I was married.

What grabs your attention most when you're looking at quilts? The color combination is almost always the first thing that I see, and then I begin to study the pattern as an afterthought. That doesn't surprise me, given that I pretty much see color first in almost everything I am drawn to.

What's your favorite occasion that causes people to gather around your table? Hands down, our annual Polish Christmas dinner celebration, Vigilia is by far my favorite. We celebrate on December 24, as is the Polish Christmas tradition, and we sit down when the first star can be seen. Since we don't live close by one another, it's one of the only times that our whole family comes together each year.

Name one thing you always like to have on your table. Fresh flowers, for sure, whether it's sunflowers and dashes in the summer, fall foliage in autumn, holly and pine at Christmas, bulbs in a small terra-cotta pot in early spring, or little garden and herb bouquets any time of the year, flowers are a breath of fresh air and loveliness no matter the season or the bouquet.

FigTreeandCompany.com

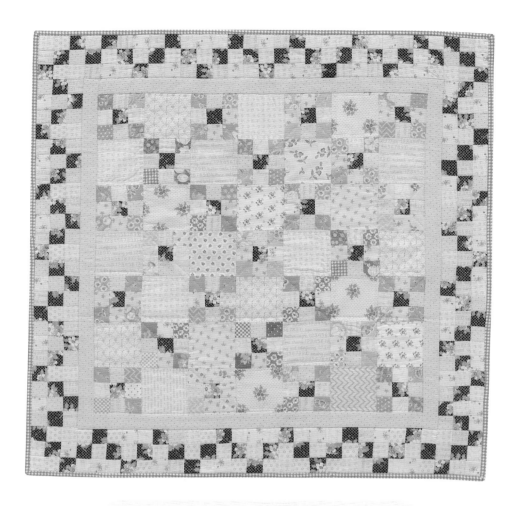

Designed and made by
JOANNA FIGUEROA

4 Join 12 A segments and 11 B segments, noting the orientation of the B segments, to make a border strip measuring 3½" × 23½", including seam allowances. Repeat to make a total of four strips.

Make 4 border strips,
3½" × 23½".

5 Add a corner block to each end of the remaining two of the border strips from step 4 to make the top and bottom borders. Each strip should measure 3½" × 29½", including seam allowances.

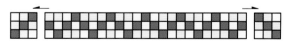

Make 1 top border,
3½" × 29½".

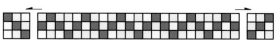

Make 1 bottom border,
3½" × 29½".

Assembling the Table Topper

1 Refer to the table-topper assembly diagram to lay out the blocks and cream 3½" squares in seven rows, alternating the blocks and squares in each row and from row to row. Sew the pieces in each row together. Join the rows to make a table-topper center measuring 21½" square, including seam allowances.

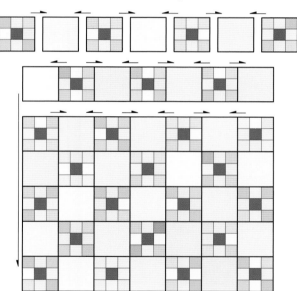

Table-topper assembly

2 Refer to the border diagram at right to sew the cream dot 1½" × 21½" strips to opposite sides of the table topper. Sew the cream dot 1½" × 23½" strips to the top and bottom edges. The table topper should measure 23½" square, including seam allowances.

3 Sew the pieced side borders to opposite sides of the table topper, noting the position of the

dark squares. Sew the pieced top and bottom borders to the top and bottom edges. The table topper should measure 29½" square.

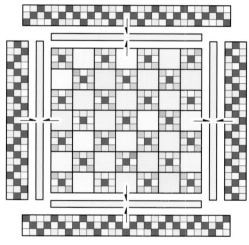

Adding the borders

Finishing the Table Topper

For more details on any finishing steps, visit ShopMartingale.com/HowtoQuilt for free downloadable information.

1 Layer the quilt top with batting and backing; baste the layers together.

2 Quilt by hand or machine. The table topper shown is machine quilted in the ditch along the seamlines using a sashiko machine to replicate the look of big-stitch hand quilting.

3 Use the gingham 2¼"-wide strips to make binding. Attach binding to the table topper.

Apple Butter

Add a touch of sweetness to your table with softly colored prints and bouquets of delicately embroidered flowers. The design is also perfect for a bedroom.

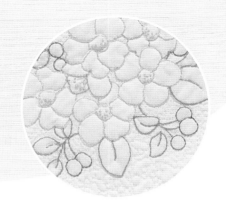

BRENDA RIDDLE

FINISHED TABLE TOPPER
40" × 40"
FINISHED BLOCK
9" × 9"

Materials

Yardage is based on 42"-wide fabric.

1⅛ yards of cream tone on tone for blocks, setting pieces, and checkerboard border
¼ yard *each* of 2 pink and 2 green prints for blocks
⅝ yard of light green print for inner border and binding
⅓ yard of blue dot for checkerboard border
⅝ yard of cream floral for outer border
2⅝ yards of fabric for backing
46" × 46" piece of batting
Water-soluble fabric marker
Embroidery hoop
Size 9 embroidery needle

Embroidery Floss

Colors listed below are for Cosmo 6-strand embroidery floss.

Light apricot (852) for flower petals
Apricot (853) for flower petals
Yellow (700) for flower centers
Dark apricot (855) for berries
Meadow green (631) for leaves and stems

Cutting

All measurements include ¼"-wide seam allowances.

From the cream tone on tone, cut:
1 strip, 4" × 42"; crosscut into 8 squares, 4" × 4"
2 strips, 2" × 42"; crosscut into 4 strips, 2" × 20"
5 strips, 1⅝" × 42"
1 square, 14" × 14"; cut into quarters diagonally to yield 4 side triangles
1 square, 10" × 10"
2 squares, 7¼" × 7¼"
4 squares, 3½" × 3½"

From *each* of the pink and green prints, cut:
1 strip, 4" × 42"; crosscut into:
    2 squares, 4" × 4" (8 total)
    1 strip, 2" × 20" (4 total)

From the light green print, cut:
4 strips, 1¼" × 42"; crosscut into:
    2 strips, 1¼" × 27½"
    2 strips, 1¼" × 26"
5 strips, 2¼" × 42"

From the blue dot, cut:
5 strips, 1⅝" × 42"

From the cream floral, cut:
4 strips, 4½" × 42"; crosscut into:
    2 strips, 4½" × 40"
    2 strips, 4½" × 32"

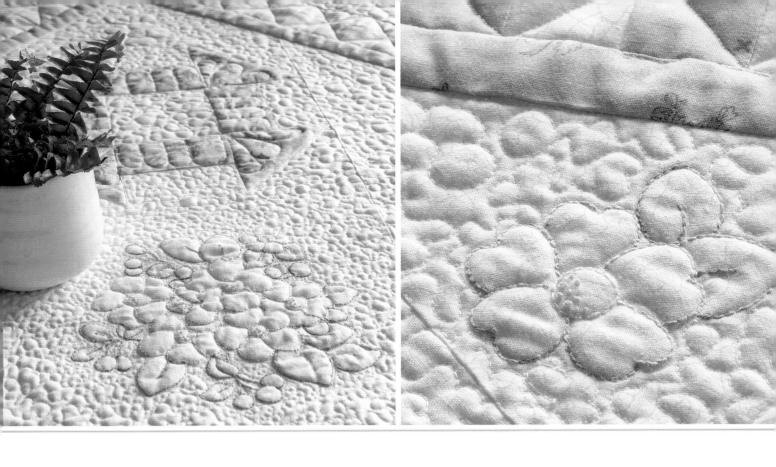

Making the Blocks

Press all seam allowances in the direction indicated by the arrows.

1 Draw a diagonal line from corner to corner on the wrong side of each cream 4" square. Layer a marked square on a pink 4" square, right sides together. Sew ¼" from both sides of the drawn line. Cut the unit apart on the marked line to make two half-square-triangle units. Trim the units to measure 3½" square, including seam allowances. Repeat to make four units from each pink print (eight total).

3½"

3½"

Make 4 of each
pink print (8 total).

2 Repeat step 1 using the remaining marked squares and the green 4" squares. Make four units from each green print (eight total).

3½"

3½"

Make 4 of each
green print (8 total).

3 Sew a cream 2" × 20" strip to each pink and green 2" × 20" strip to make four strip sets. Each strip set should measure 3½" × 20", including seam allowances. Cut each strip set into four segments, 3½" square (16 total).

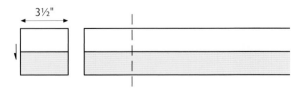

3½"

Make 1 strip set, 3½" × 20",
from each pink and green print (4 total).
Cut each strip into 4 segments, 3½" × 3½".

4 Lay out four matching pink half-square-triangle units, four pink segments from step 3 that match the half-square-triangle units, and one cream 3½" square in three horizontal rows. Sew the pieces in each row together. Join the rows to make a block. Make two pink blocks and two green blocks measuring 9½" square, including seam allowances.

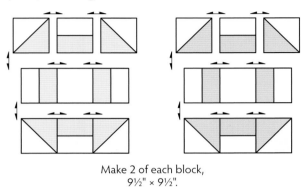

Make 2 of each block,
9½" × 9½".

Embroidering the Design

Use two strands of floss and the embroidery needle to stitch the designs.

1 Using the water-soluble marker, center and trace the bouquet design on page 42 onto the right side of the cream 10" square.

2 Draw a diagonal line from corner to corner on the right side of each cream 7¼" square. Lightly mark a scant ¼" seam allowance on both sides of the marked line and around the outer edges of each square. Trace the corner flower design on page 42 onto the right side of each marked triangle.

3 For the bouquet and corner flowers, use the light apricot and apricot floss to backstitch the flower petals. Use the dark apricot floss to backstitch the berries. Use the meadow green floss to backstitch the leaves and stems. Use the yellow floss to backstitch around the flower centers and make French knots inside the flower centers.

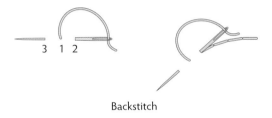

Backstitch

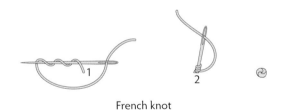

French knot

4 Place a towel on your pressing surface. Lay each embroidered square right side down on the towel and press carefully.

5 Trim the embroidered bouquet square to measure 9½" square.

6 Cut each of the embroidered corner flower squares in half diagonally to yield four corner triangles.

Designed and made by
BRENDA RIDDLE

Making the Checkerboard Border

1 Sew a cream 1⅝"-wide strip to a blue dot strip to make a strip set that measures 2¾" × 42", including seam allowances. Repeat to make a total of five strip sets. From the strip sets, cut 104 segments, 1⅝" × 2¾".

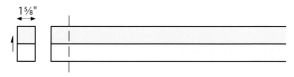

Make 5 strip sets, 2¾" × 42".
Cut 104 segments, 1⅝" × 2¾".

2 Join 24 segments, rotating every other segment, to make a side border. Repeat to make a total of two borders measuring 2¾" × 27½", including seam allowances.

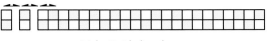

Make 2 side borders,
2¾" × 27½".

3 Join 28 segments, rotating every other segment, to make a top border. Repeat to make the bottom border. The borders should measure 2¾" × 32", including seam allowances.

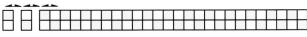

Make 2 top/bottom borders,
2¾" × 32".

Assembling the Table Topper

1 Refer to the quilt assembly diagram below to lay out the blocks, embroidered center square, cream side triangles, and embroidered corner triangles in diagonal rows as shown in the table-topper assembly diagram below. Sew the pieces into rows. Join the rows, matching the seam intersections. Add the corner triangles last.

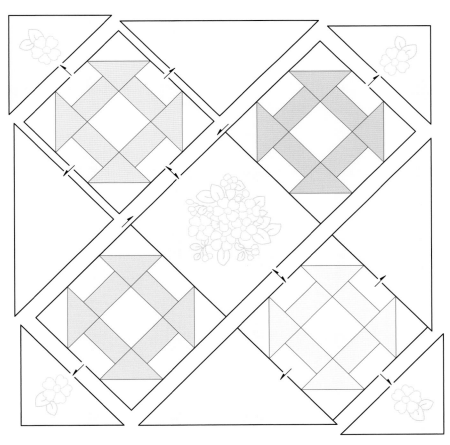

Table-topper assembly

2 Trim and square up the table-topper top, making sure to leave ¼" beyond the points of all blocks for seam allowances. The table-topper top should measure 26" square, including seam allowances.

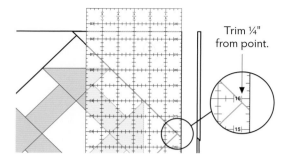

Trim ¼"
from point.

3 Refer to the border diagram below to sew the light green 1¼" × 26" strips to opposite sides of the table topper. Sew the light green 1¼" × 27½" strips to the top and bottom edges. The table topper should measure 27½" square, including seam allowances.

4 Sew the 27½"-long checkerboard borders to opposite sides of the table topper. Sew the 32"-long checkerboard borders to the top and bottom edges. The table topper should measure 32" square, including seam allowances.

5 Sew the cream floral 4½" × 32" strips to opposite sides of the table topper. Sew the cream floral 4½" × 40" strips to the top and bottom edges. The table topper should measure 40" square.

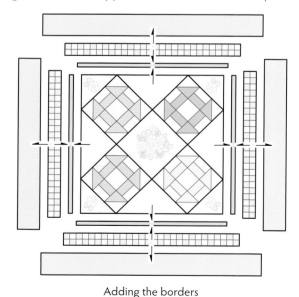

Adding the borders

Finishing the Table Topper

For more details on any finishing steps, visit ShopMartingale.com/HowtoQuilt for free downloadable information.

1 Layer the table-topper top with batting and backing; baste the layers together.

2 Quilt by hand or machine. The table topper shown is machine quilted in the ditch along all the seamlines. The blocks are quilted with a fan design in the triangles and humps in the rectangles. A meandering design is quilted in the background of the blocks, the setting triangles and center square, and the outer border. Diagonal lines are quilted across the squares in the checkerboard border to create a diagonal grid.

3 Use the light green 2¼"-wide strips to make binding and then attach the binding to the table topper.

A Perfect Fit

I admit—I love pieced borders. I also admit that they can be a little tricky, as the finished pieced border section needs to finish to a very specific size. But don't let that stop you from adding such a special touch to your quilt!

If for some reason the inner portion of the quilt is a little bigger (or smaller) than the pattern calls for, use the solid inner border to help make some adjustments to the size of the quilt. If your quilt center is a little too big, trim a little from the width of the inner border to make it the size it should be. In the same way, if the quilt center is a little smaller than it should be, you can make the inner border strips a little wider to make the quilt the size it should be. (That little inner border can give you the wiggle room you just might need!)

Table Talk
BRENDA RIDDLE

How many chairs are around your most-often-used table? My breakfast table usually has four chairs but can easily accommodate more!

If you could sit around the table with two or three other quilters, who would they be and why? I would love to sit around the table with my grandmas. They both were quilters and were called home before I started quilting. I have some of the quilts they made (such treasures!). I would love to sit and share our admiration and appreciation for this wonderful craft.

What's something you know you do differently from most people? I'm left-handed, so I do a lot of things differently! One thing I do that has nothing to do with being left-handed is that I can wear the same thing daily and I'm just fine with that. (In fact I love the simplicity of it!)

Describe your favorite way to set your table. I like to set it buffet-style, where folks can help themselves (and maybe indulge more on their favorites!).

What grabs your attention most when you're looking at quilts? I think it's the use of color. Color creates the mood of a quilt and helps me appreciate a quilt that is outside of my usual comfort zone.

What's your favorite occasion that causes people to gather around your table? Family reunions. The older I am, the more I treasure the times with family gathered.

When was the last time you tried something new and what was it? Last spring, I found out there was a sugar-free version of Chick-fil-A's lemonade, and I gave it a try. Oh, my! It's so good.

Name one thing you always like to have on your table. Flowers, always flowers.

When quilting a small project: I usually use quilting that's a little more compact on a table topper because I think it helps keep the topper flat, so decorative items placed on it stay more balanced.

BrendaRiddleDesigns.com

Corner flower embroidery pattern

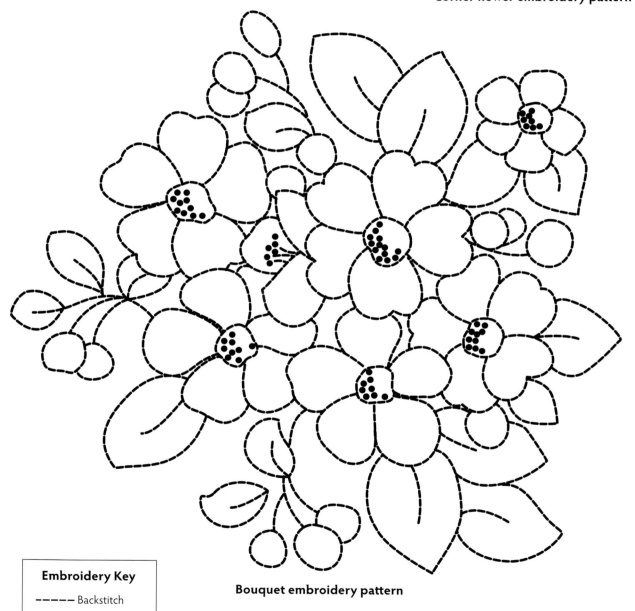

Bouquet embroidery pattern

Embroidery Key

----- Backstitch

● French knot

Home for Christmas

Can you imagine the houses on Candy Cane Lane? Peek into the windows of each cookie-cutter house for fussy-cut holiday trees that will delight your guests.

ANNE SUTTON

FINISHED TABLE RUNNER
18½" × 42½"
FINISHED STAR BLOCK
4" × 4"
FINISHED APPLIQUÉ BLOCK
9" × 16"

Materials

Yardage is based on 42"-wide fabric.

⅛ yard of cream solid for Star blocks
⅓ yard of red check for Star blocks, appliqué, and border
¼ yard of red holly print for Star blocks and appliqué
¼ yard of cream stripe for appliqué background
½ yard of red stripe for appliqué blocks, appliqués, border, and binding
⅛ yard of gray print for appliqué blocks
⅜ yard of cream print for center background
6" × 6" square *each* of 3 gray prints and 1 cream Christmas tree print for appliqués
6" × 9" rectangle of red print for appliqués
1⅜ yards of fabric for backing
25" × 49" piece of batting
Red embroidery floss
Size 9 embroidery needle

Cutting

All measurements include ¼"-wide seam allowances.

From the cream solid, cut:
2 strips, 1½" × 42"; crosscut into:
    16 rectangles, 1½" × 2½" (A)
    16 squares, 1½" × 1½" (D)

From the red check, cut:
3 strips, 1½" × 42"; crosscut into:
    2 strips, 1½" × 40½"
    24 squares, 1½" × 1½" (B)

From the red holly print, cut:
1 strip, 1½" × 42"; crosscut into 24 squares, 1½" × 1½" (C)

From the cream stripe, cut:
1 strip, 6½" × 42"; crosscut into 2 rectangles, 6½" × 16½"

From the red stripe, cut:
2 strips, 1½" × 42"; crosscut into:
    2 strips, 1½" × 18½"
    2 strips, 1½" × 16½"
4 strips, 2¼" × 42"

From the gray print, cut:
1 strip, 2½" × 42"; crosscut into 2 strips, 2½" × 16½"

From the cream print, cut:
1 strip, 6½" × 42"; crosscut into 4 rectangles, 6½" × 9½"
1 strip, 4½" × 42"; crosscut into:
    1 rectangle, 4½" × 6½"
    4 rectangles, 3" × 4½"
    2 rectangles, 1½" × 4½"

Making the Star Blocks

Press all seam allowances in the direction indicated by the arrows.

1 Draw a diagonal line from corner to corner on the wrong side of 16 B and 16 C squares. Place a marked B square on the left end of an A rectangle, right sides together. Sew on the marked line. Trim the excess corner fabric ¼" from the stitched line. Place a marked C square on the opposite end of the A rectangle. Sew and trim as before to make a flying-geese unit that measures 1½" × 2½", including seam allowances. Repeat to make a total of eight units. Using the remaining marked squares, repeat to make eight reversed units, reversing the position of the B and C squares.

Make 8 of each unit,
1½" × 2½".

2 Lay out two B and two C squares in two horizontal rows of two squares each. Sew the squares in each row together. Join the rows to make a four-patch unit. Repeat to make a total of four units measuring 2½" square, including seam allowances.

Make 4 units,
2½" × 2½".

3 Lay out two flying-geese units, two reverse flying-geese units, one four-patch unit, and four D squares in three horizontal rows. Sew the pieces in each row together. Join the rows to make a Star block. Repeat to make a total of four blocks measuring 4½" square, including seam allowances.

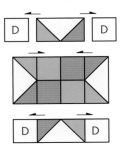 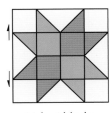

Make 4 blocks,
4½" × 4½".

Making the Appliqué Blocks

1 Using the patterns on page 49 and referring to the photo on page 47 for fabric placement, use your preferred appliqué method to prepare two trees, two tree trunks, six houses, six doors, six windows, six roofs, six chimneys, and 10 stars from the appropriate fabrics, centering the Christmas tree motif within the window shapes.

2 Referring to the appliqué placement diagram, place half of the shapes on a cream stripe rectangle, aligning the bottom of the houses, doors, and tree trunk with the edge of the rectangle. Appliqué in place. Repeat to appliqué the remaining shapes to the second cream stripe rectangle.

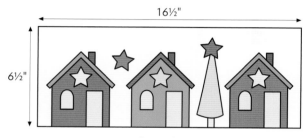

16½"

6½"

Appliqué placement

3 Stem-stitch the window lines using two strands of red floss and the embroidery needle.

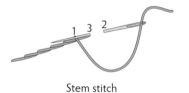

Stem stitch

★ Sew Invisible!

If you own a Bernina sewing machine, use the invisible appliqué stitch (it's stitch 3 on my machine, but models vary) when sewing your appliqué to the backgrounds. It's the perfect stitch for machine appliqué! Other machine brands may have a similar stitch, so be sure to look in your owner's manual.

4 Sew a red stripe 1½" × 16½" strip to the top of an appliquéd unit. Sew a gray print strip to the bottom of the unit to make a block measuring 9½" × 16½", including seam allowances. Repeat to make a total of two appliquéd blocks.

Make 2 blocks,
9½" × 16½".

Assembling the Table Runner

1 Join two cream print 6½" × 9½" rectangles, two cream print 3" × 4½" rectangles, and one Star block to make a row. Make two rows measuring 9½" × 16½", including seam allowances.

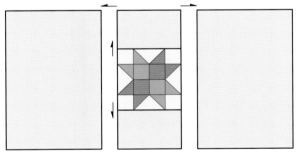

Make 2 rows,
9½" × 16½".

2 Join two cream print 1½" × 4½" rectangles, two Star blocks, and the cream print 4½" × 6½" rectangle to make a row measuring 4½" × 16½", including seam allowances.

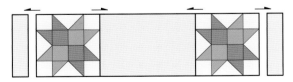

Make 1 row,
4½" × 16½".

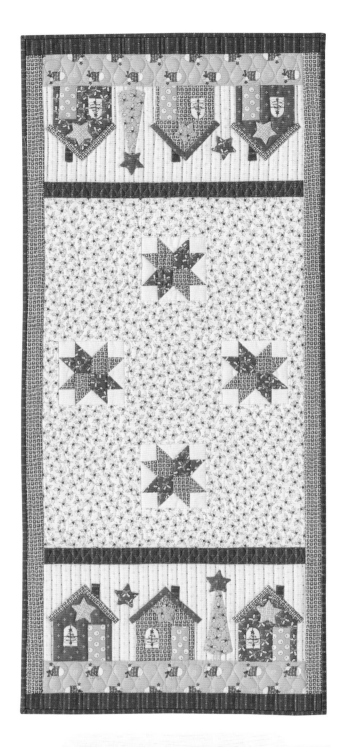

Designed by ANNE SUTTON;
pieced by NANCY RITTER;
quilted by MAGGI HONEYMAN

Table Talk
ANNE SUTTON

How many chairs are around your most-often-used table? None. My most-used table is my cutting table in the center of my studio. Standing room only!

If you could sit around the table with two or three other quilters, who would they be and why? I can think of at least 10 people I'd love to be sitting with, but if I list them and leave someone out, I'll be in big trouble, so I'll choose someone no longer with us. I would have loved to be sitting with Sue Garman, chatting about appliqué and design techniques. I love everything she created!

Describe your favorite way to set your table. I set my table with different china to fit the occasion and then serve buffet-style. It's a combination of fancy and casual.

What grabs your attention most when you're looking at quilts? If the quilt has appliqué, that's what I'll look at first. If it's a pieced quilt, then it's the colors.

What's your favorite occasion that causes people to gather around your table? I like any celebration that brings my family together, but my favorite has to be Christmas Day. It takes me all week to get ready, but I love it!

When was the last time you tried something new and what was it you tried? I love to try new recipes. I rate them by "This would be good for . . ." and I name the celebration.

Name one thing you always like to have on your table. Good food.

When quilting a small project: Don't overdo the quilting. Small calls for simple.

BunnyHillDesigns.com

3 Refer to the table-runner assembly diagram below to lay out the appliqué blocks, the two rows from step 1, and the row from step 2. Join the rows to make a table-runner center measuring 16½" × 40½", including seam allowances.

4 Sew the red check 1½" × 40½" strips to the long edges of the table runner. Sew the red stripe 1½" × 18½" strips to the short ends of the table runner. The table runner should measure 18½" × 42½".

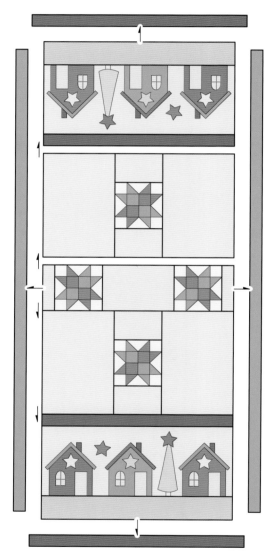

Table-runner assembly

Finishing the Table Runner

For more details on any finishing steps, visit ShopMartingale.com/HowtoQuilt for free downloadable information.

1 Layer the table-runner top with batting and backing; baste the layers together.

2 Quilt by hand or machine. The table runner shown is machine quilted in the ditch around the appliqués and along the seamlines. A ribbon candy design is quilted in the gray strips. Swirls and loops are quilted in the background.

3 Use the red stripe 2¼"-wide strips to make binding and then attach the binding to the table runner.

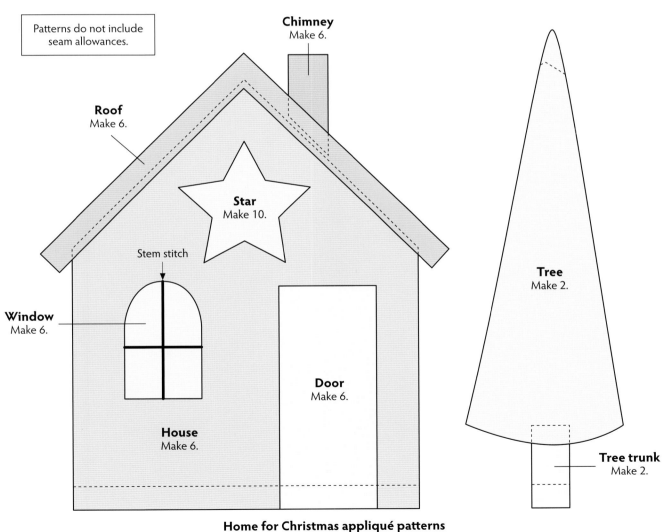

Patterns do not include seam allowances.

Chimney
Make 6.

Roof
Make 6.

Star
Make 10.

Stem stitch

Window
Make 6.

Door
Make 6.

House
Make 6.

Tree
Make 2.

Tree trunk
Make 2.

Home for Christmas appliqué patterns

Add It Up

You don't have to be a math whiz to know that easy-to-make Plus blocks and cheerful fabrics add up to a winning table runner.

COREY YODER

FINISHED TABLE RUNNER
12½" × 36½"
FINISHED BLOCK
3" × 3"

Materials

Yardage is based on 42"-wide fabric.

16 squares, 5" × 5", of assorted prints for blocks

⅔ yard of white solid for blocks, setting squares, and border

¼ yard of gray diagonal stripe for binding

½ yard of fabric for backing

19" × 43" piece of batting

12-weight gray thread for hand quilting (optional)

Cutting

All measurements include ¼"-wide seam allowances.

From *each* of the assorted prints, cut:

2 squares, 1½" × 1½" (32 total)

1 rectangle, 1½" × 3½" (16 total)

From the white solid, cut:

3 strips, 1½" × 42"; crosscut into 64 squares, 1½" × 1½"

2 strips, 3½" × 42"; crosscut into 17 squares, 3½" × 3½"

3 strips, 2" × 42"; crosscut into:
  2 strips, 2" × 36½"
  2 strips, 2" × 9½"

From the gray diagonal stripe, cut:

3 strips, 2¼" × 42"

Making the Blocks

Press all seam allowances in the direction indicated by the arrows.

1 Join one print square and two white 1½" squares to make a unit. Repeat to make a total of two matching units measuring 1½" × 3½", including seam allowances.

Make 2 units,
1½" × 3½".

2 Sew the units from step 1 to opposite sides of a matching print rectangle to make a block measuring 3½" square, including seam allowances.

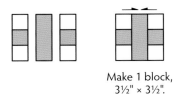

Make 1 block,
3½" × 3½".

3 Repeat steps 1 and 2 to make a total of 16 blocks.

Assembling the Table Runner

1 Lay out the blocks and white 3½" squares in 11 horizontal rows. Sew the blocks and squares in each row together. Join the rows to make a table-runner center measuring 9½" × 33½", including seam allowances.

Table Talk
COREY YODER

How many chairs are around your most-often-used table? Four.

If you could sit around the table with two or three other quilters, who would they be and why? I have so much fun spending time with my fellow Moda designers. I would happily spend an afternoon or more with any of them!

Describe your favorite way to set your table. I am so not fancy, it's sort of fend for yourself at our house. Grab a plate out of the cupboard and utensils out of the drawer, serve yourself some food buffet-style, and find a seat!

What grabs your attention most when you're looking at quilts? The colors always catch my eye first.

What's your favorite occasion that causes people to gather around your table? My mom, sisters, and I have a "sip and chat." We get together, drink coffee or tea, maybe have a snack, and just chat. It's such a nice way to spend a morning.

When was the last time you tried something new and what was it? In May 2020, I started running or walking at least 5K every day. (You'll have to ask me when this book comes out if I've kept at it!)

Name one thing you always like to have on your table. Usually I'm pretty happy if my table does not have everyone's things on it—my husband's computer, my daughter's art supplies, homework, water bottles, mugs, you name it!

When quilting a small project: Remember they're great for trying new techniques, such as a new free-motion-quilting design or hand quilting. They're also ideal for trying out a new technique such as appliqué or pieced curves.

CorianderQuilts.com

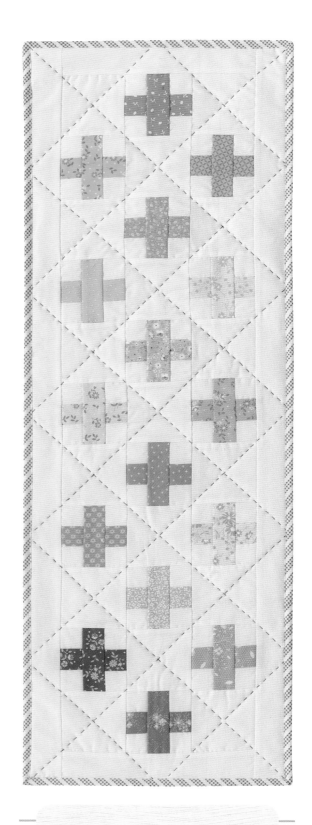

Designed and made by
COREY YODER

2 Sew the white 2" × 9½" strips to the short ends of the table runner. Sew the white 2" × 36½" strips to the long edges. The table runner should measure 12½" × 36½".

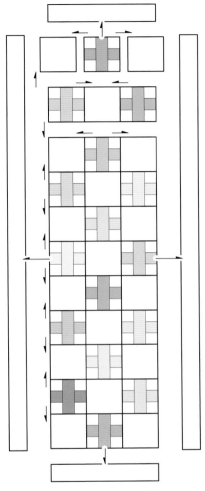

Table-runner assembly

Finishing the Table Runner

For more details on any finishing steps, visit ShopMartingale.com/HowtoQuilt for free downloadable information.

1 Layer the table-runner top with batting and backing; baste the layers together.

2 Quilt by hand or machine. The table runner shown is hand quilted with straight lines and a big stitch to create a diagonal grid.

3 Use the striped 2¼"-wide strips to make binding and then attach the binding to the runner.

FINEST

5 LBS. NET

QUALITY

© ampfire

REG. U S PAT OFF

WHITE

Marshmallows

Made By THE CAMPFIRE CO. Milwaukee US

Let it Snow

Let It Snow

Because of its simple block construction, stitching up the runner is a cinch! Add a little fusible raw-edge appliqué, and then get your shovel ready to scoop up the compliments!

LYNNE BOSTER HAGMEIER

FINISHED TABLE RUNNER
18½" × 40½"
FINISHED BLOCK
2" × 2"

Materials

Yardage is based on 42"-wide fabric. Fat eighths measure 9" × 21".

8 fat eighths of assorted navy prints for blocks
⅞ yard of tan print for blocks and appliqués
⅝ yard of navy print for border and binding
1⅜ yards of fabric for backing
25" × 47" piece of batting
½ yard of 17"-wide paper-backed fusible web
Thread to match appliqués

Cutting

All measurements include ¼"-wide seam allowances.

From *each* of the navy print fat eighths, cut:
3 strips, 1½" × 21"; crosscut into 28 squares,
   1½" × 1½" (224 total)

From the tan print, cut:
8 strips, 2½" × 42"; crosscut into 112 squares,
   2½" × 2½"

From the navy print yardage, cut:
1 strip, 4½" × 42"; crosscut into 2 strips,
   4½" × 18½"
2 strips, 2½" × 32½"
4 strips, 2¼" × 42"

Making the Blocks

Press all seam allowances in the direction indicated by the arrows.

Draw a diagonal line from corner to corner on the wrong side of each navy square. Place marked squares on opposite corners of a tan square, right sides together. Sew on the marked lines. Trim the excess corner fabric ¼" from the stitched lines. Make 112 blocks measuring 2½" square, including seam allowances.

Make 112 blocks,
2½" × 2½".

Perfect Connecting Corners

Connecting corners are a simple way to add triangles to the corners of a block without using templates. After drawing and stitching on the diagonal line, test accuracy by pressing the navy square toward the corner. If the 90° corners do not line up perfectly, try stitching a thread-width closer to the corner for perfect corners every time.

Table Talk

LYNNE BOSTER HAGMEIER

How many chairs are around your most-often-used table? Six.

If you could sit around the table with two or three other quilters, who would they be and why? Barb Groves, Mary Jacobson, and Lisa Bongean, because they're all smart cookies who always make me laugh!

What's something you know you do differently from most people? I prefer anything worn and old over things that are shiny and new.

Describe your favorite way to set your table. I've been collecting Rae Dunn pottery in black and white. I love the words on the dishes—Dinner, Hangry, Let's Eat, Share, Family, etc. When there's a crowd, everyone loves to pick their plate or bowl. It makes me smile.

What grabs your attention most when you're looking at quilts? Color.

What's your favorite occasion that causes people to gather around your table? The 4th and 5th of July (my birthday). We can't all get together at the same time at Christmas, but July 5th is always a family affair!

When was the last time you tried something new and what was it? We started a vegetable garden this year. It's been so fun and rewarding.

Name one thing you always like to have on your table. For me, it's a quilted runner and something vintage for a centerpiece.

When quilting a small project: I use a size 60 needle and Aurifil 50-weight thread. When stitching in the ditch, the thread simply disappears!

KTQuilts.com

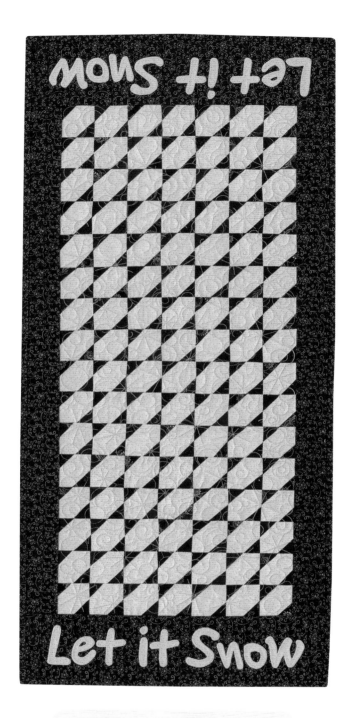

Designed by
LYNNE BOSTER HAGMEIER;
pieced and quilted by JOY JOHNSON

56

Assembling the Table Runner

1 Lay out the blocks in 16 rows of seven blocks each as shown in the table-runner assembly diagram below. Sew the blocks into rows. Join the rows to make a table-runner center measuring 14½" × 32½", including seam allowances.

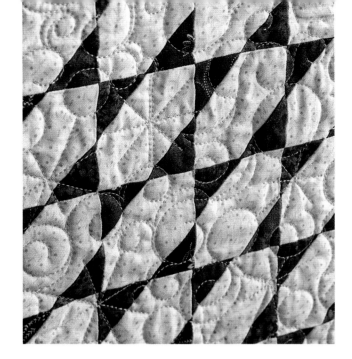

Table-runner assembly

2 Sew the navy 2½" × 32½" strips to the long edges of the table runner. Sew the navy 4½" × 18½" strips to the ends of the table runner. Press the seam allowances toward the navy strips. The table runner should measure 18½" × 40½".

3 Using the patterns on page 58, trace each shape twice onto the fusible web. Roughly cut out each shape, about ½" beyond the drawn line. Follow the manufacturer's instructions to fuse each shape to the wrong side of the tan print. Cut out each shape on the marked line and remove the paper backing.

4 Position the letters on each end of the table runner to spell out "Let it Snow." Fuse the appliqués in place. Topstitch about ⅛" from the outer edge of each letter using matching thread.

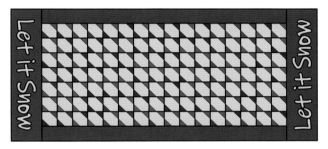

Appliqué placement guide

Finishing the Table Runner

For more details on any finishing steps, visit ShopMartingale.com/HowtoQuilt for free downloadable information.

1 Layer the table-runner top with batting and backing; baste the layers together.

2 Quilt by hand or machine. The table runner shown is machine quilted in the center with an allover loop-and-stars design. Straight lines are quilted in the border.

3 Use the navy 2¼"-wide strips to make binding and then attach binding to the table runner.

Patterns do not include seam allowances and are reversed for fusible appliqué.

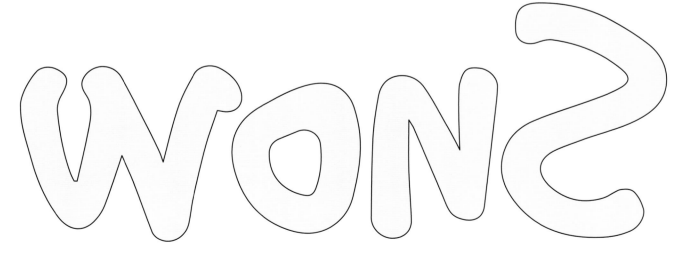

Make 2 of each shape.

Frank's Prairie

Art meets architecture on a Frank Lloyd Wright–inspired table runner. Customize the size by adjusting the length of the center rectangles to fit your table.

ROBIN PICKENS

FINISHED TABLE RUNNER
14" × 66½"

Materials

Yardage is based on 42"-wide fabric.

¼ yard of green floral for center section
⅛ yard of aqua print for center section
1⅛ yards of white tone on tone for center
   and end sections
¼ yard of green print for end sections
½ yard of cream print for binding
1¼ yards of fabric for backing
20" × 73" piece of batting

Cutting

All measurements include ¼"-wide seam allowances.

From the green floral, cut:
2 strips, 3½" × 20½"

From the aqua print, cut:
3 strips, 1" × 20½"

From the white tone on tone, cut:
2 strips, 2½" × 42"; crosscut into:
    8 rectangles, 2½" × 2¾"
    4 rectangles, 2" × 2½"
    16 rectangles, 1¼" × 2½"
5 strips, 1½" × 42"; crosscut into:
    12 rectangles, 1½" × 5½"
    6 rectangles, 1½" × 4"
    12 rectangles, 1½" × 3¼"
    16 rectangles, 1½" × 1¾"
2 strips, 5½" × 42"; crosscut into 8 rectangles,
    5½" × 6"
2 strips, 3½" × 42"; crosscut into:
    2 strips, 3½" × 20½"
    4 rectangles, 2½" × 3½"
2 strips, 2" × 42"; crosscut into:
    4 rectangles, 2" × 10½"
    2 rectangles, 2" × 4"

From the green print, cut:
2 squares, 4" × 4"
12 squares, 2½" × 2½"
14 squares, 1½" × 1½"
2 rectangles, 1" × 10½"
4 rectangles, 1" × 2½"

From the cream print, cut:
5 strips, 2¼" × 42"

Making the Center Section

Press all seam allowances in the direction indicated by the arrows.

Join the green floral strips, aqua strips, and white 3½" × 20½" strips to make the center section. The section should measure 14" × 20½", including seam allowances.

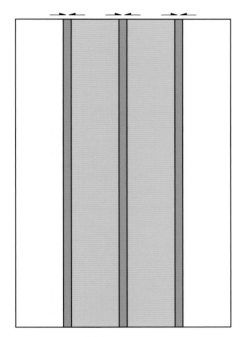

Make 1 section,
14" × 20½".

Making the End Sections

1 Join white 2" × 10½" rectangles to the long sides of a green 1" × 10½" rectangle. Repeat to make a total of two units measuring 4" × 10½", including seam allowances.

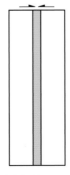

Make 2 units,
4" × 10½".

2 Sew white 1¼" × 2½" rectangles to opposite sides of a green 2½" square. Repeat to make a total of four units measuring 2½" × 4", including seam allowances.

Make 4 units,
2½" × 4".

3 Sew white 1½" × 1¾" rectangles to opposite sides of a green 1½" square. Repeat to make a total of two units measuring 1½" × 4", including seam allowances.

Make 2 units,
1½" × 4".

4 Sew a green 4" square to one end of a unit from step 1. Lay out the joined unit with three white 1½" × 4" rectangles, two units from step 2, and one unit from step 3 as shown. Join the pieces and a white 2" × 4" rectangle to make unit A. Make two units measuring 4" × 23½", including seam allowances.

Unit A.
Make 2 units,
4" × 23½".

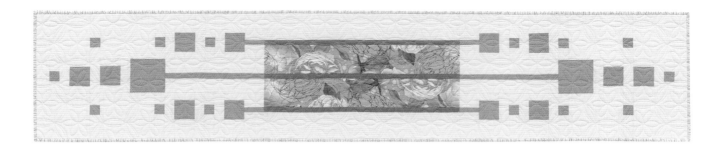

Designed by ROBIN PICKENS;
pieced by ROBIN PICKENS and SUSAN VAUGHN;
quilted by ROBIN PICKENS

5 Join one white 2½" × 3½" rectangle, one green 1" × 2½" rectangle, and one white 2" × 2½" rectangle. Repeat to make a total of four units measuring 2½" × 5½", including seam allowances.

Make 4 units,
2½" × 5½".

6 Join one white 2½" × 2¾" rectangle, one green 2½" square, and one white 1¼" × 2½" rectangle. Repeat to make a total of eight units measuring 2½" × 5½", including seam allowances.

Make 8 units,
2½" × 5½".

7 Join one white 1½" × 3¼" rectangle, one green 1½" square, and one white 1½" × 1¾" rectangle. Repeat to make a total of 12 units measuring 1½" × 5½", including seam allowances.

Make 12 units,
1½" × 5½".

8 Lay out three white 1½" × 5½" rectangles, two white 5½" × 6" rectangles, one unit from step 5, two units from step 6, and three units from step 7. Join the pieces to make unit B. Repeat to make a total of two units measuring 5½" × 23½", including seam allowances. In the same manner, make two of unit C, reversing the orientation of the units from steps 5–7.

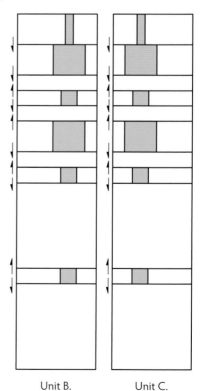

Unit B.   Unit C.

Make 2 of each unit,
5½" × 23½".

9 Sew a B unit to the left edge of an A unit. Sew a C unit to the right edge of the A unit to make an end section. Repeat to make a total of two sections measuring 14" × 23½", including seam allowances.

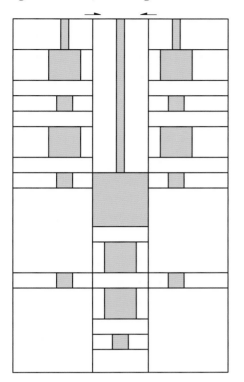

Make 2 sections,
14" × 23½".

Change the Size

This runner is easy to adjust for different table sizes. By extending or shortening the center rectangles you can adjust the length as needed. You can also shorten the thin line sashing unit within the center row of the end sections and subtract that same amount from the white 6"-long rectangles on the sides to make the ends shorter.

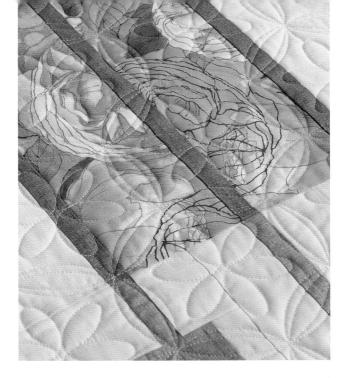

Assembling the Table Runner

Lay out the center and end sections as shown in
the table-runner assembly diagram. Join the sections,
making sure to match the seam intersections.
The table runner should measure 14" × 65½".

Finishing the Table Runner

For more details on any finishing steps, visit
ShopMartingale.com/HowtoQuilt for free
downloadable information.

1 Layer the table-runner top with batting and
backing; baste the layers together.

2 Quilt by hand or machine. The table runner
shown is machine quilted with an allover
floral design.

3 Use the cream 2¼"-wide strips to make binding
and then attach the binding to the table runner.

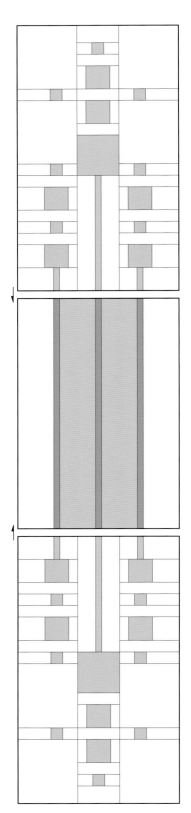

Table-runner assembly

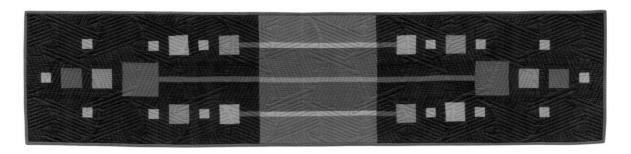

*For this alternate colorway, Robin reversed the position of the light
and dark fabrics and used warm colors rather than cool ones. She also
shortened the center section so the finished length would fit her space.*

Table Talk
ROBIN PICKENS

How many chairs are around your most-often-used table? We have four around a round table. Since one daughter is off to school, three are usually used.

If you could sit around the table with two or three other quilters, who would they be and why? I'd love to sit with Jen Kingwell and also Brigitte Heitland of Zen Chic. I really look forward to seeing them at Quilt Markets as they're both fascinating, lovely women. They also both have a style with piecing, color, and composition that I love. I've made quilts from patterns by each of them!

What's something you know you do differently from most people? I like to plan on my computer before sewing. I enjoy making color studies on the computer to see the variations I can achieve with color and contrast. But, that's also why I love making improv quilts—it provides balance to the planned projects.

Describe your favorite way to set your table. Because our dining table has such a pretty walnut grain, I prefer a table runner over a tablecloth. Dinner parties are a fun time to use my different sets of silver salt-and-pepper shakers, vintage butter knives, and olive forks from thrift-store shopping.

What's your favorite occasion that causes people to gather around your table? We usually entertain with simple dinner parties with one or two other couples. No special occasion required!

Name one thing you always like to have on your table. I usually have large bowls in the center of my kitchen and dining room tables. I keep fruit in them, or just enjoy the shape and color of the bowl. It's one of the reasons I designed my pattern with a large center panel so there's a logical place for a centerpiece bowl.

When quilting a small project: I like to think about the room where it will be used. My house is fairly modern, so I lean toward quilting motifs for that aesthetic.

RobinPickensInc.com

Sidewalk Gossip

The word is out—rows of squares are joined into four identical quadrants, then joined with a row of sashing. It's easier than it looks!

SUSAN ACHE

FINISHED TABLE TOPPER
42½" × 42½"

Materials

Yardage is based on 42"-wide fabric.

⅛ yard of blue tone on tone for squares (A)

½ yard of white print for squares (B)

1 yard of aqua tone on tone for squares, border, and binding (C)

¼ yard of chartreuse print for squares (D)

⅔ yard of navy floral for squares (E)

½ yard of gray tone on tone for squares (F)

⅜ yard of aqua solid for squares (G)

½ yard of chartreuse solid for squares (H)

¼ yard of aqua floral for squares (I)

⅛ yard of aqua print for squares (J)

2¾ yards of fabric for backing

49" × 49" piece of batting

Cutting

All measurements include ¼"-wide seam allowances.

From the blue tone on tone (A), cut:

1 strip, 1½" × 42"; crosscut into 17 squares, 1½" × 1½"

From the white print (B), cut:

8 strips, 1½" × 42"; crosscut into 196 squares, 1½" × 1½"

From the aqua tone on tone (C), cut:

1 strip, 1½" × 42"; crosscut into 20 squares, 1½" × 1½"

3 strips, 3" × 42"*

2 strips, 3" × 37½"

5 strips, 2¼" × 42"

*If your fabric width measures at least 42½", you'll only need 2 strips. Cut each of these strips 3" × 42½".

From the chartreuse print (D), cut:

3 strips, 1½" × 42"; crosscut into 72 squares, 1½" × 1½"

From the navy floral (E), cut:

13 strips, 1½" × 42"; crosscut into 336 squares, 1½" × 1½"

From the gray tone on tone (F), cut:

9 strips, 1½" × 42"; crosscut into 212 squares, 1½" × 1½"

From the aqua solid (G), cut:

7 strips, 1½" × 42"; crosscut into 160 squares, 1½" × 1½"

From the chartreuse solid (H), cut:

9 strips, 1½" × 42"; crosscut into 232 squares, 1½" × 1½"

From the aqua floral (I), cut:

4 strips, 1½" × 42"; crosscut into 92 squares, 1½" × 1½"

From the aqua print (J), cut:

2 strips, 1½" × 42"; crosscut into 32 squares, 1½" × 1½"

Designed and pieced by SUSAN ACHE;
quilted by SUSAN ROGERS

Assembling the Table Topper

Press all seam allowances in the direction indicated by the arrows.

1 Referring to the diagram, lay out the following 1½" squares in 18 rows of 18 squares each. Sew the squares into rows. Join the rows to make a quadrant. Repeat to make a total of four quadrants measuring 18½" square, including seam allowances.

- 4 A squares
- 46 B squares
- 4 C squares
- 16 D squares
- 80 E squares
- 50 F squares
- 38 G squares
- 56 H squares
- 22 I squares
- 8 J squares

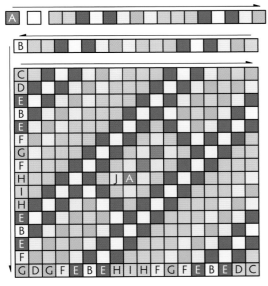

Make 4 quadrants,
18½" × 18½".

2 Join three B, one C, two D, four E, three F, two G, two H, and one I square to make a sashing unit. Repeat to make a total of four units measuring 1½" × 18½", including seam allowances.

Make 4 units,
1½" × 18½".

Table Talk
SUSAN ACHE

How many chairs are around your most-often-used table? We have four chairs around our regular family table and 12 chairs when everyone's here.

If you could sit around the table with two or three other quilters, who would they be and why? Sandy Klop (I want to know her secrets for making cool, detailed, vintage-looking quilts); Jen Kingwell (I want to know how she works so many prints together effortlessly without overthinking every single block); and Barbara Brackman (who wouldn't want her on your team for a "name that quilt block" game?).

What's something you know you do differently from most people? I take apart fat-quarter bundles, untie Jelly Rolls, Layer Cakes, and Honey Buns, and sort them all by color rather than collection.

Describe your favorite way to set your table. China and cloth napkins are my go-to, and we always serve family-style at the big table.

What grabs your attention most when you're looking at quilts? Always color first and then how a quilt is set. I love blocks for fillers over sashing. I'll stop in my tracks for pieced borders.

What's your favorite occasion that causes people to gather around your table? All holidays and celebrations, little or big, are held at my house. When our kids were little, it was easier to send the kids to their rooms than it was for us to leave a family function.

When was the last time you tried something new and what was it? I try something new in every quilt I make. I never want to repeat the same thing over and over again.

Name one thing you always like to have on your table. All our holidays are planned by spinning the globe. The country is chosen months in advance so everyone can research the food and plan accordingly! So, my table never has the same things for any occasion.

Instagram: @yardgrl60

3 Lay out the four quadrants, four sashing units, and one A square in three rows, rotating the quadrants and units as shown in the table-topper assembly diagram below. Sew the pieces into rows. Join the rows to make a table-topper center measuring 37½" square, including seam allowances.

4 Sew aqua C 3" × 37½" strips to opposite sides of the table-topper center. Join the aqua C 3" × 42" strips end to end. From the pieced strip, cut two 3" × 42½" strips. Sew these strips to the top and bottom edges of the table topper. The table topper should measure 42½" square.

Finishing the Table Topper

For more details on any finishing steps, visit ShopMartingale.com/HowtoQuilt for free downloadable information.

1 Layer the table-topper top with batting and backing; baste the layers together.

2 Quilt by hand or machine. The table topper shown is machine quilted with an allover diagonal grid.

3 Use the aqua C 2¼"-wide strips to make binding and then attach the binding to the table topper.

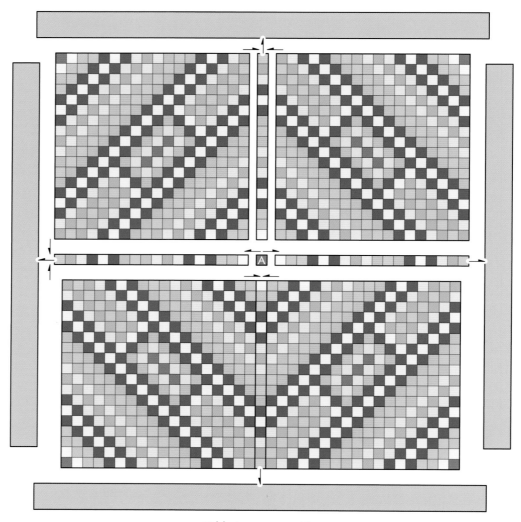

Table-topper assembly

Teatime Trio

Afternoon tea has never looked better! English paper piece a hexagon topper and matching coasters in a delightful set to adorn your teatime table.

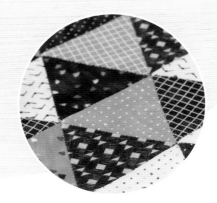

JANET CLARE

FINISHED SIZES
5½" × 4¾" (small coaster);
11" × 9½" (medium coaster);
16½" × 14¼" (topper)

Materials

Yardage is based on 42"-wide fabric. Fat eighths measure 9" × 21".

5 fat eighths of assorted indigo prints for triangles
3 fat eighths of assorted green prints for triangles
4 fat eighths of assorted cream prints for triangles
½ yard of cream wool for backings
Cardstock or lightweight cardboard for templates

Cutting

All measurements include ¼"-wide seam allowances.

From *each* of the indigo prints, cut:
2 strips, 4" × 21"; crosscut into 8 squares, 4" × 4"
   (40 total; 1 is extra)

From *each* of the green prints, cut:
1 strip, 4" × 21"; crosscut into 5 squares, 4" × 4"
   (15 total)

From *each* of the cream prints, cut:
2 strips, 4" × 21"; crosscut into 8 squares, 4" × 4"
   (32 total; 2 are extra)

Making the Coasters and Topper

Instructions are for making all three items.

1 Trace the triangle pattern on page 75 onto the template material to make 84 triangle templates. Cut out each template on the marked line.

2 Pin a triangle template to the wrong side of each indigo, green, and cream square. Cut out each fabric shape, adding a generous ¼" seam allowance all around the paper template. Fold the seam allowance over the edge of the template. Use a needle and thread to hand baste the seam allowances to the template, stitching through all the layers and making sharp folds at each point. Or, use a fabric glue stick to glue baste the seam allowances to the templates. The folding will create tails; leave the tails hanging out as shown. Make 39 indigo, 15 green, and 30 cream triangles.

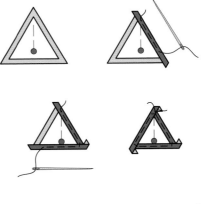

Make 39 units.   Make 15 units.   Make 30 units.

71

Designed and made by
JANET CLARE

3 Thread a needle with a single strand of thread and tie a knot in one end. Place one indigo and one green triangle right sides together. Whipstitch them together from corner to corner, catching only the folded edges. Do not stitch through the paper.

Whipstitch.

4 Repeat step 3 to join a total of three indigo and three green triangles as shown, alternating colors to make the small coaster.

Make 1 small coaster.

Soothing Stitches

Hand stitching can be very soothing and meditative, especially if you make an occasion of it. Good-quality tools that you enjoy using play a big part in the pleasure of sewing, so treat yourself to a new needle, fine thread, and small sharp scissors; really notice and appreciate your tools each and every time you use them.

Then light a candle, play your favorite film or music, pour a refreshing drink, and settle in for an hour or so of enjoying the colors and prints and the feel of your needle and thread slipping smoothly through the fabric.

5 In the same way, join nine indigo, three green, and 12 cream triangles to make the medium-sized coaster. You can stitch the triangles together in rows or start from a central triangle and work out toward the edges.

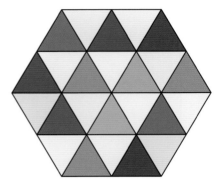

Make 1 medium coaster.

6 Join 27 indigo, nine green, and 18 cream triangles to make the table topper.

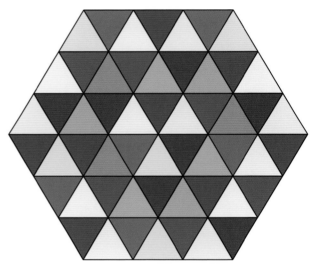

Make 1 large coaster.

7 Press the topper and coasters, snip the basting threads, and remove the paper templates. Templates can be reused in another project, if desired.

Finishing the Coasters and Topper

1 Using the pieced tops as guides, add 1" all around the perimeter of each one and cut a small, medium, and large hexagon from the cream wool.

2 Pin or hand baste a pieced top in the center of a same-size wool hexagon, wrong sides together. Slip-stitch around the outer edges of the pieced top. Trim the wool backing, leaving about ⅛" beyond the edges of the coaster or topper.

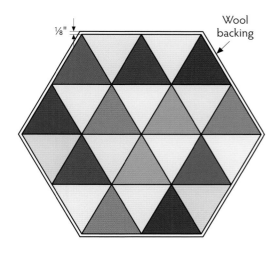

⅛"

Wool backing

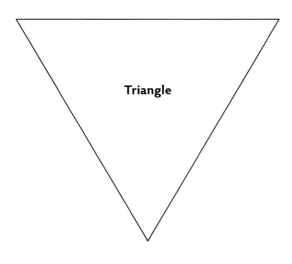

Triangle

Pattern does not include seam allowance.

Table Talk
JANET CLARE

How many chairs are around your most-often-used table? Four.

If you could sit around the table with two or three other quilters, who would they be and why? All the Moda folks, please!

Describe your favorite way to set your table. My favorite table would have a tablecloth, mismatched china, a cake stand, pastry forks, and cloth napkins, all set for afternoon tea.

What grabs your attention most when you're looking at quilts? The pattern is what catches my eye first.

What's your favorite occasion that causes people to gather around your table? Birthday breakfast is the occasion I enjoy.

When was the last time you tried something new and what was it? Most recently I tried vegan brownies.

Name one thing you always like to have on your table. A well-dressed table deserves a tablecloth, in my book!

JanetClare.co.uk

Scramble

Got a scrap pile you're itching to use? Mix and match light and dark pieces in a striking design of simple half-square-triangle units stitched in two sizes. It radiates beauty!

BETSY CHUTCHIAN

FINISHED TABLE TOPPER
27½" × 27½"
FINISHED BLOCK
4½" × 4½"

Materials

Yardage is based on 42"-wide fabric.

1 yard *total* of assorted light prints for blocks
1 yard *total* of assorted dark prints for blocks
¼ yard of red print for single-fold binding
1 yard of fabric for backing
32" × 32" piece of batting

Cutting

All measurements include ¼"-wide seam allowances.

From the assorted light prints, cut a *total* of:
18 squares, 4" × 4"; cut in half diagonally to make
    36 triangles
90 squares, 2½" × 2½"

From the assorted dark prints, cut a *total* of:
18 squares, 4" × 4"; cut in half diagonally to make
    36 triangles
90 squares, 2½" × 2½"

From the red print, cut:
3 strips, 1¼" × 42"

Making the Blocks

Press all seam allowances in the direction indicated by the arrows.

1 Sew a dark and a light 4" triangle together along the long diagonal edges to make a large half-square-triangle unit. Trim the unit to measure 3½" square, including seam allowances. Repeat to make a total of 36 units.

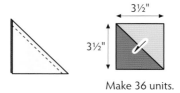

Make 36 units.

2 Draw a diagonal line from corner to corner on the wrong side of each light 2½" square. Layer a marked square on a dark 2½" square, right sides together. Sew ¼" from both sides of the drawn line. Cut the unit apart on the marked line to make two small half-square-triangle units. Trim the units to measure 2" square, including seam allowances. Repeat to make a total of 180 units.

Make 180 units.

Designed and made by
BETSY CHUTCHIAN

3 Join two small half-square-triangle units, noting the orientation of the units. Make 36 A units measuring 2" × 3½", including seam allowances.

Make 36 A units,
2" × 3½".

4 Join three small half-square-triangle units, noting the orientation of the units. Make 36 B units measuring 2" × 5", including seam allowances.

Make 36 B units,
2" × 5".

5 Lay out one A unit, one B unit, and one large half-square-triangle unit from step 1, noting the orientation of the units. Sew the A unit to the left edge of the large half-square-triangle unit. Sew the B unit to the top edge to make a block. Make 36 blocks measuring 5" square, including seam allowances.

Make 36 blocks,
5" × 5".

Lay-Flat Seams

Once you've made all the half-square-triangle units, arrange them on a design wall or table following the quilt layout. Move the parts around until you're pleased with the way the prints and colors are distributed. Then pick up the pieces for one block at a time, sew them together, press, and return to the layout.

Consider twisting the intersection where triangles meet and clipping next to the seam allowance to reduce bulk in that one spot. (See "Clipping Trick" on page 95 for details.)

Table Talk
BETSY CHUTCHIAN

How many chairs are around your most-often-used table? Four.

If you could sit around the table with two or three other quilters, who would they be and why? Wow, just two or three? Jan Patek, because I'm a long-time fan of her primitive, folk-art appliqué style; Lisa Bongean because I love wool appliqué, and her embroidery is gorgeous; and Jen Kingwell because she hand pieces beautifully. Busy hands make beautiful work.

What's something you know you do differently from most people? I like to cut and sew just one block at a time.

Describe your favorite way to set your table. I like to use dishes that match the season or holiday. Adding a tablecloth, cloth napkins, and a pretty centerpiece finishes the setting.

What grabs your attention most when you're looking at quilts? Fabric always get my attention, lots and lots of fabric.

What's your favorite occasion that causes people to gather around your table? Holidays! Halloween and Christmas parties and dinners are my favorite times to gather with friends and family.

Name one thing you always like to have on your table. A small quilt and an arrangement of seasonal or holiday items are what you'll find on many tables in my home.

When quilting a small project: I keep the quilting simple and let the fabrics shine. That's especially true for table toppers that I plan to decorate with objects on top.

BestsysBestQuiltsandMore.blogspot.com

Assembling the Table Topper

Lay out the blocks in six rows of six blocks each, rotating the blocks as shown. Sew the blocks into rows. Join the rows to make a table topper measuring 27½" square.

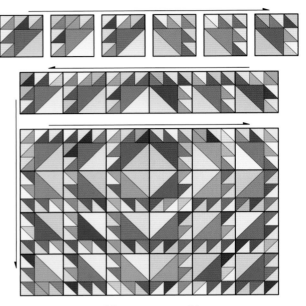

Table-topper assembly

Finishing the Table Topper

For more details on any finishing steps, visit ShopMartingale.com/HowtoQuilt for free downloadable information.

1 Layer the table-topper top with batting and backing; baste the layers together.

2 Quilt by hand or machine. The table topper shown is machine quilted with horizontal, vertical, and diagonal straight lines established by the small half-square-triangle units.

3 Use the red print 1¼"-wide strips to make single-fold binding and then attach the binding to the table topper.

Homeward Bound

Don't let this flock of flying geese intimidate you. They'll stack up quickly and easily when you follow the instructions for making four at a time.

APRIL ROSENTHAL

FINISHED TABLE RUNNER
16½" × 32½"
FINISHED BLOCK
2" × 4"

Materials

Yardage is based on 42"-wide fabric.

⅓ yard of cream print A for blocks

32 squares, 5" × 5", of assorted medium and dark prints for blocks (referred to collectively as "dark")

16 squares, 5" × 5", of assorted light and medium prints for blocks (referred to collectively as "light")

⅓ yard of cream print B for sashing and border

¼ yard of navy stripe for binding

⅝ yard of fabric for backing

17" × 37" piece of batting

Plan Ahead

Before cutting, choose 16 dark 5" squares that contrast with cream A. Label the dark squares as C and set aside. Pair the 16 light 5" squares with the 16 remaining dark 5" squares to contrast. Choose color and scale of fabrics that are very different. Decide which square will be the background (sky) and which will be the goose triangle. Label background squares as D. Label squares for goose triangles as E.

Cutting

All measurements include ¼"-wide seam allowances.

From cream A, cut:
4 strips, 1⅞" × 42"; crosscut into 64 squares, 1⅞" × 1⅞"

From cream B, cut:
4 strips, 2½" × 32½"

From *each* of the 16 C squares, cut:
1 square, 3¼" × 3¼" (16 total)

From *each* of the 16 D squares, cut:
4 squares, 1⅞" × 1⅞" (64 total)

From *each* of the 16 E squares, cut:
1 square, 3¼" × 3¼" (16 total)

From the navy stripe, cut:
3 strips, 2¼" × 42"

Making the Blocks

Press all seam allowances in the direction indicated by the arrows.

1 Draw a diagonal line from corner to corner on the wrong side of each cream A square. Align two squares on opposite corners of a C square, right sides together. The marked squares should overlap in

the center. Sew ¼" from both sides of the drawn line. Cut the unit apart on the drawn line to make two units.

2 Place a marked square on the corner of the larger triangle from a step 1 unit, right sides together, noting the direction of the marked line. Sew ¼" from both sides of the drawn line. Cut the unit apart on the drawn line. Repeat with the remaining marked square and unit from step 1 to yield four flying-geese units. The units should measure 1½" × 2½", including seam allowances. Repeat to make 16 sets of four matching units (64 total).

Make 16 sets of
4 matching units,
1½" × 2½".

3 Draw a diagonal line from corner to corner on the wrong side of each D square. Repeat steps 1 and 2 using the D and E squares to make 16 sets of four matching units (64 total).

Make 16 sets of
4 matching units,
1½" × 2½".

4 Join four matching flying-geese units to make a block. Repeat to make a total of 32 blocks measuring 2½" × 4½", including seam allowances.

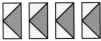

Make 32 blocks,
2½" × 4½".

Table Talk
APRIL ROSENTHAL

How many chairs are around your most-often-used table? Six chairs at our dining table, but four more matching chairs around the house for when we have people over to play games and share food!

If you could sit around the table with two or three other quilters, who would they be and why? My great-great-grandma, whom I never met; I have quilts she hand stitched, and I'd love to learn more about her. I also always enjoy spending time with Vanessa Goertzen of Lella Boutique and Chelsi Stratton—they keep me laughing and sane!

What's something you know you do differently from most people? I'm a super-fast reader, which has helped me so much in learning new skills and languages.

Describe your favorite way to set your table. We set the table simply, with matching plates, mismatched silverware (and plastic for my youngest), a big pitcher of ice water, and simple healthy food.

What grabs your attention most when you're looking at quilts? I love small, repetitive pieces in quilts, and lots of bright happy colors! I definitely can't look away when there's a spectrum of colors and lots of precision.

What's your favorite occasion that causes people to gather around your table? Every year we host a very large Hanukkah party, even though we're Christian. My husband's father is Jewish, and we love sharing the beautiful lessons and yummy food of his heritage with our family and friends.

Name one thing you always like to have on your table. I love to have a pretty table topper with a tray and potted succulents on my table. It brings a moment of beauty and calm to my kitchen area, which is almost always full of hustle and bustle!

When quilting a small project: I like to make sure the quilting is dense enough to hold up to frequent washing and still look good after lots of use.

AprilRosenthal.com

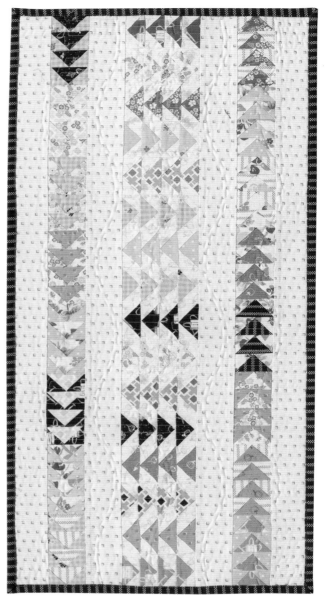

Designed and made by
APRIL ROSENTHAL

Assembling the Table Runner

1 Join eight blocks along their short ends, with all the triangles pointing in the same direction, to make a row. Repeat to make a total of two rows measuring 2½" × 32½", including seam allowances.

Make 2 rows,
2½" × 32½".

2 Join 16 blocks along their long edges, rotating every other block, to make a row. The row should measure 4½" × 32½", including seam allowances.

Make 1 row,
4½" × 32½".

3 Refer to the table-runner assembly diagram below to lay out the rows from steps 1 and 2, making sure to position the top and bottom rows so the geese point in opposite directions. Add the cream B strips, alternating them with the rows as shown. Join the rows to make a table runner measuring 16½" × 32½".

Finishing the Table Runner

For more details on any finishing steps, visit ShopMartingale.com/HowtoQuilt for free downloadable information.

1 Layer the table-runner top with batting and backing; baste the layers together.

2 Quilt by hand or machine. The table runner shown is machine quilted with a double wavy line through the cream B strips and rows of parallel straight stitching across the entire topper.

3 Use the striped 2¼"-wide strips to make binding and then attach the binding to the table runner.

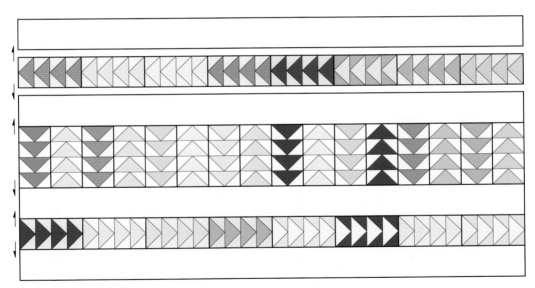

Table-runner assembly

Plymouth

Contrast is the key to turning a neutral color palette into a subtly sophisticated topper. Accent the easy-to-piece oversized block with grid quilting for added texture.

CHELSI STRATTON

FINISHED TABLE TOPPER
24½" × 24½"

Materials

Yardage is based on 42"-wide fabric.

⅞ yard of white solid for units and border
¼ yard of medium gray print for units
¼ yard of dark gray floral for units
¼ yard of light gray print for binding
⅞ yard of fabric for backing
29" × 29" piece of batting

Cutting

All measurements include ¼"-wide seam allowances.

From the white solid, cut:
1 strip, 6½" × 42"; crosscut into:
    4 squares, 6½" × 6½"
    2 squares, 6" × 6"
4 strips, 2½" × 42"; crosscut into:
    2 strips, 2½" × 24½"
    2 strips, 2½" × 20½"
1 square, 10½" × 10½"

From the medium gray print, cut:
1 strip, 6½" × 42"; crosscut into:
    2 squares, 6½" × 6½"
    2 squares, 6" × 6"

From the dark gray floral, cut:
1 strip, 6½" × 42"; crosscut into:
    2 squares, 6½" × 6½"
    4 squares, 5½" × 5½"

From the light gray print, cut:
3 strips, 2¼" × 42"

Making the Units

Press all seam allowances in the direction indicated by the arrows.

1 Draw a diagonal line from corner to corner on the wrong side of each dark gray floral 5½" square. Place marked squares on opposite corners of the white 10½" square. Sew on the marked lines. Trim the excess corner fabric ¼" from the stitched lines. Repeat on the remaining corners of the square to make a square-in-a-square unit measuring 10½" square, including seam allowances.

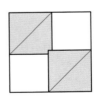
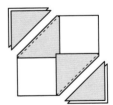
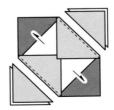
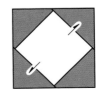

Make 1 unit,
10½" × 10½".

Designed and pieced by CHELSI STRATTON;
quilted by MARION BOTT

2 Draw a diagonal line from corner to corner on the wrong side of each white 6" square. Layer a marked square on a medium gray 6" square, right sides together. Sew ¼" from both sides of the drawn line. Cut the unit apart on the marked line to make two half-square-triangle units. Trim the units to measure 5½" square, including seam allowances. Repeat to make a total of four units.

  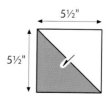

5½"

5½"

Make 4 units.

3 Draw a diagonal line from corner to corner on the wrong side of each white 6½" square. Layer a marked square on a medium gray 6½" square, right sides together. Sew ¼" from both sides of the drawn line. Cut the unit apart on the marked line to make two half-square-triangle units. Trim the units to measure 6" square, including seam allowances. Repeat to make a total of four units.

 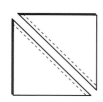 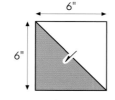

Make 4 units.

4 Repeat step 3 using the remaining marked 6½" squares and the dark gray floral 6½" squares to make four units measuring 6" square, including seam allowances.

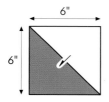

Make 4 units.

Follow the Line

To save time, you can stop marking the sewing lines on the squares and instead use Diagonal Seam Tape from Cluck Cluck Sew. This washi-style tape has a center red line (sewing line) and a perfect ¼" seamline on each side. Place the tape on your machine bed and follow the line to perfect half-square and quarter-square triangles!

5 Layer a unit from step 3 on top of a unit from step 4, right sides together with the light triangles opposing each other. Draw a diagonal line from corner to corner across the seam. Butt the diagonal seams against each other and stitch a scant ¼" seam allowance on both sides of the drawn line. Cut the squares apart on the drawn line to make two hourglass units. Trim the units to measure 5½" square, including seam allowances. Repeat to make a total of eight hourglass units.

  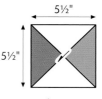

Make 8 units.

Assembling the Table Topper

1 Join two hourglass units, noting the orientation of the units, to make a side unit. Repeat to make a total of four units measuring 5½" × 10½", including seam allowances.

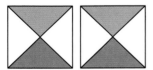 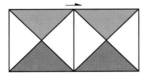

Make 4 units,
5½" × 10½".

2 Lay out the medium gray 5½" half-square-triangle units, the side units, and the square-in-a-square unit in three horizontal rows, noting the orientation of the units. Sew the units into rows. Join

the rows to make a table-topper center measuring 20½" square, including seam allowances.

Table-topper assembly

3 Sew the white 2½" × 20½" strips to opposite sides of the table topper. Sew the white 2½" × 24½" strips to the top and bottom edges. The table topper should measure 24½" square.

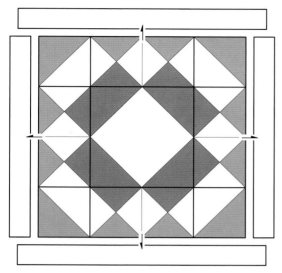

Adding the border

Finishing the Table Topper

For more details on any finishing steps, visit ShopMartingale.com/HowtoQuilt for free downloadable information.

1 Layer the table-topper top with batting and backing; baste the layers together.

2 Quilt by hand or machine. The table topper shown is machine quilted with a diagonal grid.

3 Use the light gray 2¼"-wide strips to make binding and then attach the binding to the table topper.

Table Talk
CHELSI STRATTON

How many chairs are around your most-often-used table? Six.

If you could sit around the table with two or three other quilters, who would they be and why? Definitely Vanessa Goertzen of Lella Boutique and April Rosenthal. They're like sisters to me and we always have a few good laughs together!

What's something you know you do differently from most people? I don't love chocolate, which I think is different than most people.

Describe your favorite way to set your table. Paper plates because they're easy to clean up, especially with little kids at home! We also do one fancy meal a week with plates my husband's grandmother gave us for our wedding.

What grabs your attention most when you're looking at quilts? It's a tie. The design of the quilt and the colors always stand out to me.

What's your favorite occasion that causes people to gather around your table? I love when our families get together around the table for Sunday dinners or holidays!

When was the last time you tried something new and what was it? I tried surfing out on the lake and it was so much fun!

Name one thing you always like to have on your table. Fresh veggies from my garden.

When quilting a small project: It's important to keep in mind the size and shape of your table so your topper is well proportioned to it. I also like to make different toppers for different seasons. This way, I have something fun and new on my table throughout the year.

Instagram: @chelsistratton

Cinnamon Sugar

A fanciful mix of sweet reproduction prints sprinkle across the center of a runner with understated elegance. Wrap it all up with a striped binding for the perfect finish.

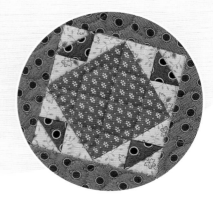

JO MORTON

FINISHED TABLE RUNNER
17¾" × 40¼"
FINISHED BLOCK
4" × 4"

Materials

Yardage is based on 42"-wide fabric.

12 squares, 6" × 6", of assorted light prints for blocks
24 squares, 5" × 5", of assorted brown and rust prints for blocks (referred to collectively as "brown")
½ yard of brown dot for setting squares and triangles
¼ yard of rust stripe for inner border and single-fold binding
1⅛ yards of black floral for outer border
1⅜ yards of fabric for backing
24" × 47" piece of batting

Cutting

All measurements include ¼"-wide seam allowances.

FOR 1 BLOCK
Each block contains 1 light and 2 brown fabrics. Repeat the cutting instructions to make 12 blocks, keeping the fabrics for each block together. When cutting the brown 3⁵⁄₁₆" squares, cut between the 3¼" and 3⅜" lines on the ruler.

From 1 light print, cut:
2 squares, 2" × 2"
4 squares, 1⅞" × 1⅞"; cut the squares in half diagonally to yield 8 triangles

From 1 brown print, cut:
2 squares, 2" × 2"

From a different brown print, cut:
1 square, 3⁵⁄₁₆" × 3⁵⁄₁₆"

FOR SETTING PIECES
From the brown dot, cut:
1 strip, 4½" × 42"; crosscut into 5 squares, 4½" × 4½"
3 squares, 7¼" × 7¼"; cut each square into quarters diagonally to yield 12 side triangles
2 squares, 4" × 4"; cut in half diagonally to yield 4 corner triangles

FOR BORDERS AND BINDING
From the rust stripe, cut:
3 strips, 1" × 42"; crosscut into:
    2 strips, 1" × 34¼"
    2 strips, 1" × 12¾"
4 strips, 1⅛" × 42"

From the *lengthwise* grain of the black floral, cut:
2 strips, 3" × 35¼"
2 strips, 3" × 17¾"

Designed and pieced by
JO MORTON;
quilted by MAGGI HONEYMAN

Making the Blocks

Press all seam allowances in the direction indicated by the arrows.

1 Select the pieces cut for one block. Draw a diagonal line from corner to corner on the wrong side of each light 2" square. Layer a marked square on a brown 2" square, right sides together. Sew ¼" from both sides of the drawn line. Cut the unit apart on the marked line to make two half-square-triangle units. Trim the units to measure 1½" square, including seam allowances. Repeat to make a total of four matching units.

Make 4 units.

2 Sew the short sides of two light triangles to the brown edges of a half-square-triangle unit. Repeat to make a total of four units.

Make 4 units.

3 Center and sew units from step 2 to opposite sides of a brown 3⁵⁄₁₆" square. Repeat on the remaining sides of the square to make a block measuring 4½" square, including seam allowances.

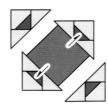

Make 1 block,
4½" × 4½".

4 Repeat steps 1–3 to make a total of 12 blocks.

Assembling the Table Runner

1 Lay out the blocks, the brown dot squares, and the brown dot side and corner triangles in diagonal rows as shown. Sew the pieces into rows. Join the rows, matching the seam intersections. Add the corner triangles last. Refer to "Clipping Trick" at right to press the seam allowances toward the setting squares and triangles.

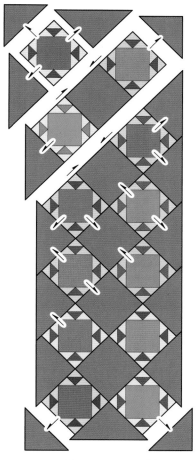

Table-runner assembly

2 Trim and square up the table-runner center, making sure to leave ¼" beyond the points of all blocks for seam allowances. The table runner should measure 11¾" × 34¼", including seam allowances.

3 Refer to the borders diagram on page 96 to sew the rust 1" × 34¼" strips to the long edges of the table runner. Sew the rust 1" × 12¾" strips to the short ends of the table runner, which should measure 12¾" × 35¼", including seam allowances.

Clipping Trick

At the intersection of the seams, clip into the seam allowance almost to the stitching on each side, ¼" from the seam (the clips will be ½" apart). The clips should be lined up with the outside edge of the seam allowance. Press the seam allowances in opposite directions and press the clipped intersection open.

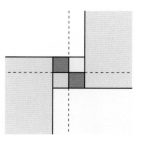

Table Talk

JO MORTON

How many chairs are around your most-often-used table? Six.

If you could sit around the table with two or three other quilters, who would they be and why? It would be my friends who helped me when I hired them to sew quilts for more than a decade. I love my friends for the people they are, besides being sewing helpers.

What's something you know you do differently from most people? I have no idea, unless it's the fact that I like to hand piece and hand quilt small quilts.

Describe your favorite way to set your table. Set dinner for two, light a candle, enjoy a glass of wine with my honey, dish up plates in the kitchen, and use cloth napkins. It's not fancy, but it sets a sharing mood.

What grabs your attention most when you're looking at quilts? Color always draws me in, or lets me pass on by.

What's your favorite occasion that causes people to gather around your table? It used to be sewing Saturdays, with the above-mentioned friends for lunch. Our home is too small for family gatherings, so we go to my sister-in-law's home for those.

Name one thing you always like to have on your table. A candle, although it's not always lit.

When quilting a small project: I like to use single-fold rather than double-fold binding. It results in less bulk around the edges and a smoother, flatter finish.

Instagram: @joquilts

4 Sew the black 3" × 35¼" strips to the long edges of the table runner. Sew the black 3" × 17¾" strips to the short ends of the table runner. The table runner should measure 17¾" × 40¼".

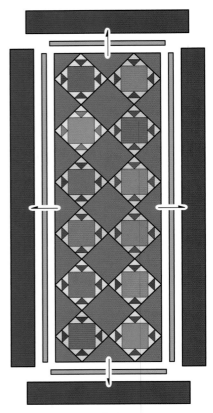

Adding the borders

Finishing the Table Runner

For more details on any finishing steps, visit ShopMartingale.com/HowtoQuilt for free downloadable information.

1 Layer the table-runner top with batting and backing; baste the layers together.

2 Quilt by hand or machine. The table runner shown is machine quilted with a diagonal grid across the blocks and outer border. A feather motif is quilted in the setting squares and triangles.

3 Use the rust 1⅛"-wide strips to make single-fold binding and then attach the binding to the table runner.